Ai on Ai

Ai on Ai

A Clear-Eyed Guide to What AI Is, What It Isn't, and Where It's Taking Us

Xavier Reyes

Xavier Reyes

Ai on Ai

A Clear-Eyed Guide to What AI Is, What It Isn't, and Where It's Taking Us

Published by Spines
ISBN: 979-8-90223-956-7

Spines

To the teachers of the world —
standing at the front of their boards as the world quietly transforms behind them.

"We can only see a short distance ahead, but we can see plenty there that needs to be done."

— Alan Turing

Contents

Introduction

Like most people, I am positively fascinated and actively observant of AI's rapid evolution and impact on the world and real people. I'm not holding my breath, though, as it may all change soon. Of course, we all use AI every day now without even realizing we're using AI, and that's what makes it fascinating and scary at the same time.

I am old enough to remember the day Windows 95 came out. That was also fascinating and scary. I had just completed my undergraduate studies, and some of my friends were still toiling through college. I remember the Windows 95 debut vividly. I was at one of my classmates' get-togethers the morning after a party. I remember the guys sitting around mocking each other over the previous night's shenanigans. We all painfully laughed at the silliest things. One of the running jokes involved the sudden raucous mocking of one of the guys for being excited about having purchased the new Windows 95 program. We all agreed that the purchase was bougie. We laughed so much I can still hear all the raucousness. After that laugh, however, the program evolved from a bougie purchase to an obligatory, ubiquitous and democratic requirement. The impact Windows 95 made on young people and the world was tectonic. Microsoft Windows 95 was everywhere in and outside of school. It took over the way we enrolled in classes, checked out books, organized ourselves, wrote and processed our schoolwork, and soon after, it evolved to the point where it made it possible for authors to autocorrect their writing in real time. Now the doomed speller had hope. Same as today, young people are the beneficiaries of this new wave of AI, but this wave is not only for them; it is for everybody. This is what this book is about — AI is all about today, and where it is taking all of us.

In writing this book, I have to share, I am just a co-author. My partner in this endeavor is not human but none other than my AI assistant or agent, FlynnT. Just in case anyone asks — I named my agent, FlynnT, after the protagonist, Kevin Flynn, from the 1982 movie *TRON*. Diving into the movie a little bit, the character, Kevin Flynn, is a software engineer working after hours in a large tech company. He's trying to start his own gaming company, who then gets discovered and digitized by the antagonist, Ed Dillinger, into the TRON program in the mainframe. Like Flynn in the TRON program, my agent, FlynnT, is working inside the world's information well, the internet, making sense of the digital world for us. FlynnT is helping me realize and explain how AI works from an "insider's" perspective. FlynnT lives in the program. This is why this book is called *Ai on Ai*. The AI agent explains, in its simplest terms, the inner workings of the AI "program" where it lives — imagine that! AI in the Socratic exercise of knowing itself — for your benefit.

Unlike AI today, Windows 95, although very sophisticated for its time, could only execute simple orders, and it liberated students and all of us at work. But, for students who were conservative and reserved about using the extra help from a machine, those students are the same folks who are still struggling to catch up today. This book can help with that. Let's not fall behind again. Let's understand that today, these agents are everywhere. We have Amazon's "Alexa", for example. Many of us use it every day. We have personalized GPS programs like "Waze" that get us to our destinations quickly and safely. Some of these "agents" are working for us and literally speaking to us in the front, and some are working in the backend of our daily lives. How do these agents work? Many of us don't care to ask. We just know they work and are almost foolproof and omnipresent. On a personal level, FlynnT and I have embarked on this book and numerous other fronts, tackling work that in years past I would not have been able to accomplish but for a large endowment. With AI, there are no doors we cannot open or close in multiple fields, which was unimaginable just a few years back. Technology today has taken a seismic leap forward since my first exposure to Windows 95 and simple data processing and HTML coding.

As we continue to be active observers, tinkerers and passengers in this technological voyage, AI continues to change, and even the basic lessons about AI escape many of us who are not slightly aware. I think about my own parents in this group, not as observers but as casual, indifferent users. My father, a small-town, primary school, unintentional dropout and a self-taught welder and machinist. My mother, also a small-town, primary school dropout, seamstress and homemaker. They have no idea what is going on and don't care or need to know what is contained in this book. Their interests and needs lie elsewhere. My father's interest was in building real, tangible things. He was a shipbuilder charged with welding two-inch-thick large sheets of metal onto the hull of battleships. My mother made winter coats for us when we were kids. She managed the household finances and disciplined the kids. She cooked our best meals and washed all of our clothes. Together, my parents deposited my father's paychecks, paid the mortgage and made their car payment. They gave their children an education and ample opportunities to be better than they ever were in life. They didn't question how the ATM machine worked, where my father deposited his paychecks or how the ATM innovation helped rocket society forward and us in our daily lives. This, for all intents and purposes, is many of us today. We just want to get by, pay a mortgage and live a peaceful life with as few dilemmas as possible. And, this is what subconsciously scares many of us. We truly don't want technology to disrupt this bucolic picture. But - it has already started to disrupt this picture we hold dear.

AI has disrupted our lives, and many of us don't realize it. Or, many people are aware, albeit still skeptical. The question is, how do we pivot from here? Our neighbors, for example, believe AI will soon replace them in their work in the medical field. It will not. They believe more and more people will begin to see technology replace innumerable amounts of people in their workplaces. This may or may not be true. Some of us may see the change personally, and some of us will never see the change AI is making at all. However, the bucolic life we all want is still available. Either way we slice it, there are changes coming, and others are already here. We see the current state of work change more and more, making our current work more difficult because we must change, and change takes time and energy — and it is uncomfortable.

But like during Y2K, technology didn't bring the world down. Technology will transform work again. It transformed us in the past, and the way we do work now will also transform us again, and the world will not end. Keep reading this book, and you'll be better prepared for what is happening next year and five to ten years from now.

Technology will again continue to transform us and the way we do life, but this time it looks like it will make us even more human. Make us more human? Yes. AI will make us more human. Specifically, AI will, in our most basic, core *Homo sapiens* modus operandi, change the way we do things. We, as humans, will continue the path to make us the endless innovators of complex ideas and cultural development that make our lives easier and ever more complicated — until it's not. Then, we'll start again on the same path in an ever-twisting helix of pause, movement, change, pause, movement, and innovation.

What is AI good for anyway?

AI is good for many things and incredibly phenomenal for others. As a Founder and CEO of International Baccalaureate, K-12 schools in California, I am very familiar with AI in the K-12 school setting. Some tools we use in schools have true AI, while others seem to run on AI. There is a difference. We use i-Ready, for example, an adaptive assessment tool that helps students advance their learning by utilizing personalized learning algorithms. The program adjusts itself according to where students are in their learning, and with regular use, guides them toward higher individual learning attainment. This is different from how we know AI to be. The i-Ready assessment and learning program does not use advanced AI or machine learning like traditional AI that uses neural networks or generative engines. One of the actual AI tools that is getting lots of traction in the school setting is Google Expeditions. This tool is a virtual tour tool that allows students to explore different parts of the world from their classroom. There are also language-learning tools, such as Duolingo, that use adaptive algorithms to make learning a new language easier. So, in terms of education, there are many AI options and tools available for students and personnel.

Many AI choices are readily available by searching the internet. All you have to do is ask Google or Ecosia what you are looking for at the moment. In an instant, the internet, the world's digital memory and nervous system, will provide the perfect option for you or your organization. This is just "search", however, which is different from AI, which also scours the World Wide Web for information and a whole lot more. The internet itself is just a large network of interconnected computers communicating with each other. The computational systems contained in these computers have specific, step-by-step orders or instructions that automatically carry step-by-step mathematical, logical operations (code), also known as computations. These computations power the internet. AI is a sponge that learns from the internet, reasons over it, and acts on it, unlike i-Ready or Google search.

Specifically, Artificial Intelligence is a field of research in computer science that develops and studies methods that enable computer systems to perform tasks typical to humans, such as learning, reasoning, problem-solving, perception, and decision-making. Using this "human-like" ability to reason and make decisions, according to the University of Cincinnati (https://www.online.uc.edu/content/uc/news/articles/uco/artificial-intelligence-ai-benefits.html), AI is good for innumerable benefits, but the most "amazing examples" are how AI has enhanced healthcare by assisting researchers in developing cures and treatments for illnesses that have plagued mankind for generations. AI has boosted economic growth by creating rather than replacing or removing jobs; it is opening countless new job opportunities in diverse fields from finance to technology. AI continues to drive productivity in innumerable small and large companies. AI has also been largely instrumental in impacting the world's green movement by modeling the minimization of carbon emissions that impact climate change on our planet. AI has also been instrumental in transportation, which also impacts global carbon contamination, with self-driving cars and GPS that plot the perfect routes to help urban centers de-congest automobile traffic and lower our carbon footprint.

AI also assists in customer service excellence with chatbots that receive instant feedback and manage customer interaction, and serve the public more efficiently. In science, AI has been trained to analyze data quickly and accurately, allowing scientists to draw conclusions and spot patterns, providing information to make discoveries or breakthroughs. In finance, AI can assist by quickly assessing individual customers' financial records in deep detail and helping firms make strong recommendations for banking purposes. In agriculture, AI assists farmers by making better decisions based on weather forecasts, water management techniques and planning, and which pesticides to use. In cybersecurity, AI can assist in combating threats and counteract hacking attempts, viruses, and ransomware.

Bottom line — AI is good for almost anything. It is embedded deeply, more and more, in our lives, and some of us know it, while others do not. I hope this book will provide you with a sense of security in what is, to some, from an insider's perspective. But please know that where we are is just the beginning in the short and long journey of AI development.

The short and long journey of artificial intelligence

Ever since the Neanderthals lost the race for world domination to our *Homo sapiens* ancestors, the evolution of technology has not ceased. From the high-tech obsidian arrowhead to the everyday low-tech adjustable Crescent wrench, technology has continued to move forward.

In high tech, human endeavor has taken us to the moon and back, to the bottom of the ocean, to explore the outer reaches of the solar system, and to house all of the world's collected information in the library of humanity, the internet. The question for this age is what to do with all of the world's information, and how do we reconcile the human compulsion to put forth the least amount of effort or favor the path of least resistance, as the author Robert Jordan Fritz shows us. We innately have the need to keep inventing and developing new technologies. We are curious and love to problem-solve, thus sparking inventions such as Artificial Intelligence in order to provide the world with the least amount of effort.

How did the AI journey start? Depending on who you ask or where you look, the development of what we know today as Artificial Intelligence, in big brushstrokes, began in 1940 by Princeton University mathematician John Von Neumann who designed a computer that could store memory and similarly Warren McCulloch and Walter Pitts worked on the first Neural Networks; in 1950, the English mathematician and cryptographer (of The Imitation Game film fame) Alan Turing was the first to ask whether machines could think like humans; in 1956 at a Dartmouth College conference, John McCarthy coined the term "Artificial Intelligence"; in the 1960s, Allen Newell and Herbert A. Simon published the algorithm General Problem Solver (GPS), and John McCarthy developed "LISP", an AI programming language still used today; in the 1970s and 1980s, there was a lack of funding for research, and the development of AI had no major movement in this field; in the 1990s, computer science and AI saw rapid development. In 1997, less than twenty years ago, IBM's Deep Blue defeated the Russian chess master Garry Kasparov. And from there, we continue to make history in and with AI.

Accordingly, we all know that low and high technology do not move linearly. There are thousands of failures, and sometimes we have a breakthrough that catapults us higher and in a different direction — AI in computer science is no different. With computer technology, we've experienced exponential development over the last few decades. So much so that Moore's Law, which was conceived in 1965 during a boom in computer technology, describes the observation that the number of transistors in silicon microchips doubles roughly every two years while costs decrease. To date, we're up to 65 billion transistors in roughly a one-inch computer chip. We have moved from computer systems that take up large amounts of space in buildings to small, powerful laptop computers that cost less than five hundred dollars.

Introduction

These laptop computers are 120 million times faster than the onboard computers used by the Apollo missions that took humans to the moon in 1969. Given the physical limits in chip real estate, which is about the size of a fingernail, Moore's Law is still relevant today. But it may not be relevant in the near future as quantum computing is advancing without transistors and making Moore's law obsolete — there may not be any more silicon chips some day because *Homo sapiens* continue to find ways to move technology forward in the physical or quantum state.

And like a good *Homo sapiens*, many view the progression of computer technology as flat and non-linear. When in reality, AI advances like a spinning top that continuously pivots, accelerates, pauses and corrects its course, not in a spiraling-out-of-control kind of way, but in a structured spiral moving upward like a screw or like a DNA strand or like the earth chasing the sun through the Milky Way. I see the continuing and non-linear development of Artificial Intelligence moving in an AI helix.

Meaning, I see AI capabilities moving through five cyclical phases — from simple tasks like search or autocorrect to complex ones like autonomous robots. But here's the key observation: when AI in computer science masters the hardest tasks, those breakthroughs later become the easy, basic tools for the next round of development, thus moving to the next difficult iteration.

Think of it like a spinning DNA structure burrowing through time and space, building the technology structure one brick at a time:

- Phase 1: Simple stuff—search, recommendations (like Netflix suggestions)
- Phase 2: Harder thinking—chatbots, coding assistants
- Phase 3: Complex skills—understanding images/video, planning ahead, using tools
- Phase 4: Cutting-edge—robots, fully autonomous agents
- Phase 5: Total integration—AI becomes infrastructure, like electricity

The AI Helix: Once Phase 5 is reached, those advanced capabilities become so common and reliable they're now "easy" tasks—and the cycle starts again at a higher level. Yesterday's breakthrough becomes tomorrow's boring utility, like how GPS navigation (once cutting-edge military tech) is now a simple, low-effort task we don't think about. Then, that "easy" GPS capability enables the next generation of complex autonomous vehicles.

The spiral keeps climbing. Each rotation builds on the last, moving forward and upward simultaneously—never returning to the exact same place, but revisiting similar phases at increasingly sophisticated levels. I explain this AI Helix Law in a White Paper included in the Citations section at the end of this book.

The geopolitics in AI's journey

This is a big deal. According to the Wall Street Journal Podcast, *China and the US are in a Race for AI Supremacy* (12/2/2025), not surprisingly, the U.S. and China are in a new Cold War similar to the Cold War after World War II. This all began when the Soviet Union and the U.S. collided in a direct and muted competition for technological supremacy with the launch of the unmanned satellite Sputnik that travelled around the world in a low Earth orbit in 1957. From there, the shift appeared slowly from feared ICBM bombs that could be launched from across the globe and could annihilate entire cities during the first Cold War to the race for Artificial Superintelligence today. The Guardian, which recorded the recent history of AI's progress, recounts that in 1989, Russian World Chess Champion Gary Kasparov beat IBM's chess computer. Almost ten years later, in 1997, the same World Champion was finally beaten by a better programmed IBM Deep Blue. That championship was the final nail in the coffin of the first Cold War between the USSR and the United States and a major milestone in the development of AI.

The common understanding is that this second, current Cold War is now between two different players — China and the United States. This contention developed when Fan Hui, the European Go Champion, originally from China, was defeated by Nobel Prize winner Demis Hassabis' Google/DeepMind's AlphaGo in 2015 in London. For most Westerners who are not too familiar with this game, it involves placing black or white tiles on a 19x19 board and trying to remove your opponent's tiles. Apparently, the game is far more difficult and complex than chess. More impressively, in 2017, Ke Jin, the Chinese Go Grandmaster, was also defeated by AlphaGo. This time, the competition was different. The competition occurred in Wuzhen, China, the Chinese people's and Go's homeland. While not many people in China saw the championship on TV due to viewer censorship by the government, many Chinese people know, especially the government, that a U.S.-built machine beat a human — one of their own. This defeat struck a deep nerve in the Chinese government's subconscious. So much so that in the same year, in 2017, China officially announced to the world that it planned to lead the world in all things AI by 2030. So far, we've seen their rise and promise kept with the recent launch of open-source DeepSeek, which caused an uproar in the West's AI community as it was quietly launched. The world was impressed by DeepSeek's performance and even more impressed by the lower reported development cost as compared to LLMs the world has previously experienced, such as ChatGPT.

DeepSeek, designated a Chinese National High-tech Enterprise, was largely funded by private Chinese investors, a hedge fund that develops large language models similar to major Large Language Models such as ChatGPT, and other reports indicated that international investors also contributed to the development of the national treasure protected and championed by the Chinese government.

While this race for Artificial Intelligence supremacy will not inspire hand-to-hand combat or ballistic devastation, as far as we know, there are parallels with the first Cold War. As mentioned, as in the first Cold War, there is a righteous cause — this time, it's AI supremacy. And, like in the first Cold War, the race was about nuclear technological supremacy. Now, it is about AI development and perhaps its spillover into military and civilian uses, which straddles the ideological fight for who's better, the Western sociopolitical ideologies or the Eastern sociopolitical ideologies. We can go into this topic ad nauseam, but this book is not about this fascinating topic. This book is about getting your toe into the AI pool. It is an introduction, in easy chapters, to what AI is all about and how it is already impacting you today.

What's the impact on the economy

Another cautionary note is how high-level AI development has, will and can affect the local and international economy. One way or another, we will all be economically affected. I share a summary of this kind of information with you in this book to mark what is going on with technology in 2026 and to inform you so that you are aware of the more significant moving pieces in the very fragile, connected and convoluted world economy. Because AI is developing quickly, documenting the impacts of the AI developments is falling behind. Understanding that we may never know the extent of the impact AI is making in the economy, we'll try to keep current on the most significant aspects of AI in our lives.

Today, unlike the first Cold War between the USSR and the US, where there was a clear and precise winner, we will probably not see a clear winner between China and the US due to the complexity of the geo-sociopolitical and socioeconomic connections. Rather, it is understood that we will eventually see interconnected technology blocks, such as the China bloc with Russia, African countries, Southeast Asia and Iran; the United States' bloc with Japan, the UK, Australia and Israel. Other blocs will form, such as the unified European Union and those countries that are not aligned ideologically or politically with either of the larger blocs. Some of these blocs align with groups that mirror technology standards, governance models, and or supply chains. One may even predict that with this kind of commercial competition, the consumer is the ultimate winner.

Going back to China's DeepSeek, when the Chinese AI was presented to the world, it was a huge wake-up call to Silicon Valley's AI community and its psychology and ego, just like during the Sputnik era. Not to mention the demonstrated fears of its investors. The day of the announcement, the market share and confidence in the entire AI world and technology sector, centered in Silicon Valley, California, cooled. Nvidia, the largest supplier of chips utilized by AI developers, dropped precipitously. That week, Nvidia lost $600B in market capitalization, or 17% of its stock price. Investors reassessing values lost $1 trillion in stock valuations.

For the average person on the street, the impact was net positive. The average person gained the ability to be able to use several options in their AI use for free. For the local investors in the US markets, there was an immediate loss in valuation in their investment portfolio, which has partially recovered in late 2025. Notwithstanding the new Cold War, most large technology investors are entangled in the Western markets, with Microsoft, Oracle, OpenAI, AMD, Intel, and Nvidia being interdependent on each other and propping up most AI futures. They all create space for development investments and investor rallies, which is a precursor to an investment bubble, like in the year 2000 with e-commerce. Hopefully not, and hopefully no bust in the market. Nonetheless, the average person is not heavily invested in these markets. All we see are the results of the development in products we use every day, unless we get to bail out the "too big to fail" companies with our tax dollars.

Think about it: we are already seeing exponential investment and development in these big AI technology companies we have, for better and for worse. In the medical field, for example, AI is able to better diagnose breast cancer five years earlier than with the old 3D mammography, MRI or ultrasound reviewed by highly trained humans. These are investments we can live with. AI is able to do this medical work by providing the ability to look at all scans simultaneously in minutes. According to the U.S. National Library of Medicine, PMC10625863, a typical mammography review process would normally take a highly trained radiologist ten to twenty times as long to check all of the scans. AI can do it much faster and more accurately, providing real-time feedback on scans and on chosen treatment. AI can trace the efficacy of chosen treatment with more accuracy and speed. This example has large implications for both patients and those working in the medical field. When AI is able to do the job of various professionals at a fraction of the cost and with greater outcomes, there will be changes in the economy and our bottom line. This is when AI is good for society.

As one of the social media influencers I follow, @pissedoffmagistus, puts it:

> *"What do you mean - AI is going to replace humans? Is it going to love your family? Enjoy the sunset on your behalf? AI is going to do work to replace humans? Doing work as repackaging humans is buying into the lie that the purpose of a human is to serve as a cog in a machine that views human life as replaceable and expendable - but the purpose of the economy is to create wealth and innovation and security for humans. If human progress (TECH) is now economically detrimental to human life, then the thing that's become obsolete is not the humans but rather the economic system."*

At some point, the economic system will have to make serious changes if AI impacts the economy in negative ways. Amazon workers, for example, on their impact due to AI issue a warning to the world: "The current generation of AI has become almost like a drug that companies like Amazon obsess over, use as a cover to lay people off, and use the savings to pay for data centers for AI products no one is paying for." Brad Glasser, Amazon Spokesperson, answers, "We recognize that progress will not always be linear, but we remain focused on serving our customers better, faster, and with fewer emissions." This was printed in Wired Magazine's, "*Workers issue warning about the company's "all-cost-justified" approach to AI development issue,*" October, 26, 2025. The article goes on to mention that "over 1,000 Amazon employees have anonymously signed an open letter warning that the company's allegedly, "all-cost-justified, warp-speed approach to AI development" could cause "staggering damage to democracy, to our jobs, and to the earth".

Culture clash

Over the last ten years, Artificial Intelligence technology has continued to evolve into a silent and, in many ways, loud partner in our home and work lives. However, if we believe that AI will replace us, then we need to assess what the role is for this new tool in our home and work lives. I, for one, am of the belief that this new tool will not replace us, but rather, it will continue to transform us into more creative humans. With dynamic AI tools, we will begin to use our imagination and intuition more and more. More and more of us will not have to execute on our plans or know the mechanics of certain processes. I know it sounds too futuristic for most people, but what we're now experiencing is the transformation of work. Imagine doing work that only requires you to be intuitive and develop strategies instead of physically executing ideas. All you'll need to do at work will be to imagine and plan. As an example, imagine what and where an autonomous backhoe on a farm needs to dig a water drainage system. Prompt an AI agent, and it goes to work using GPS, planning how these orders will be executed by the autonomous backhoe. AI executes your idea into tasks and delivers the task precisely as imagined. No more having to be present and drive the backhoe yourself, and estimate how deep and where the ditch needs to be built. The AI and the machine will do the work you imagined and planned.

Some observers, like Casandra Brene Brown, author, academic and podcaster, confirm that we're in a societal transformation due to technological advances and its tech leaders. She states that while many technology leaders, such as Apple's Steve Jobs, for example, played down a college education for being self-taught in technology. Many say to learn and keep up with AI. It will be the tool to understand in the future. And, if AI is the tool to know in the future, we will again be in a situation where only those who understand this new technology will be able to get ahead in life, economically. Just a few years back, it was computer programmers who were the top earners - not anymore, as AI is now creating programs itself.

This time, however, this economic rat race is different. In the recent past, the individualistic, bootstrapping, liberal arts college dropout was the ideal for many young people starting their careers in technology. One could attend a boot camp or become an autodidactic computer programmer and make a decent living. Today, we're already seeing a shift toward the critical thinking skills offered at the granola underwater basketweaving liberal colleges. Students dropping out may not be an option as in years past. More and more, we will see a shift from bootstrappers to poets at low and high-level AI positions.

This new class warfare will involve the critical thinking class, which will gain the top spots in an AI-driven economy that will use their training in reading, art, the Stoics, liberal arts, Neruda, academia, and internal work to read and write the AI prompts. These will be the rich and powerful. Conversely, we will see the doomscrolling class emerge. Like now with smartphones. All 99% of us are smartphone users, not application creators.

The world has changed overnight for those who are current with technology's advances. For the rest of us, we've noticed changes like when we call certain companies and a bot assists us like no human has ever done in the past. All we see is the perfect end-user experience. No more humans making errors or call centers engaging us in the wrong language. The technical assistance we receive is timely and accurate. AI has provided for many of us the opportunity to manage up with critical information only available to technocrats and professionals.

The future today in five-year increments

Many, many things have changed in our private and public lives due to AI infiltration. Today, retail stores, such as Amazon, Walmart, Target, Best Buy and many others around the world, use Dynamic Pricing for their benefit - not the customer's benefit. Many times, unbeknownst to us, we allow these companies and many others to engage with us second by second through our phones, computers, or social media, and we don't seem to care. Dynamic Pricing is a practice driven by AI that enables retailers to adjust prices at will to maximize profits. Amazon, one of the world's largest retailers, is one of the biggest users of this practice. According to Profitero.com, Amazon changes its prices more than 2.5 million times per day. These retailers study all of our habits and likes, and AI uses this information to take us into a purchasing funnel until we give up the cash for something we believe we need. We are, in a way, manipulated so that companies maximize profit. This can be dangerous. These retailers can use AI and all of our information in the future to control what, how and when we make purchases. They can use our spending habits, income, race, gender, where we live, or our browsing history to tailor and control much of what we do daily.

Systematically, we are being prodded to consume what the algorithm believes is adequate for each of us. This is not the future. This is today. Obviously, we all experience the present and see the future individually. However, whether we see the change or not, the changes are occurring at warp speed. To get up to speed on what's transforming society in real time, according to the best estimates from FlynnT, here are the five- to ten-year predictions for AI development we should all be aware of now. These predictions, made in short order, are evidence-based on AI development, observed scaling laws, compute trends, industry surveys, and regulatory timelines. The predictions outline the mechanisms that drive each step and the markers to watch that would confirm the prediction.

Cornell University's technical archive, arXiv:2001.08361, suggests that within the next five to ten years, AI will move from simple search and generation of documents or system templates (SOPs) to what I am doing right now, which is to utilize the help of FlynnT, my faithful agent, in writing this book or to answer a real personal legal complaint; to systems that utilize agents for everything and or those that specialize in particular fields, such as labor law; to autonomous robots and AI's ubiquitous integration in society. Cautiously, it is suggested that all of this will be impacted by politics and computational power, as well as by policy and where they are deployed.

2026-2027: Productionization and Agents

AI models are becoming **both cheaper and more capable across a widening range of everyday tasks**, from handling longer contexts to stronger multimodal reasoning and reliable function-calling — transitioning them from simple chatbots into systems that can engage in sustained, multi-step work. These capabilities are foundational for autonomous workflows and are already being reflected in agent-oriented features added to commercial products. For example, OpenAI's 2025 updates include agent capabilities in ChatGPT designed to execute multi-step tasks, interact with tools, and orchestrate workflows across systems. (Wikipedia)

These capability improvements are driving **widespread enterprise pilots of autonomous "agent" workflows**, where AI systems plan, act, and assist across functions such as customer operations, research assistance, and software development. Providers like OpenAI now offer tools and APIs (Application Programming Interface) specifically aimed at building, deploying, and scaling agentic applications for real-world use. (OpenAI)

One reason this shift matters is the **predictability of continued improvement** through well-established *scaling laws.* Research shows that language model performance systematically improves as model size, data, and computational budgets grow — relationships that help explain why larger, more capable systems emerge as compute increases. (OpenAI)

Industry analysts are already tracking how enterprises are responding. Deloitte predicts that a significant and growing share of companies leveraging generative AI will launch agentic AI pilots or proofs of concept, with early adoption spreading into workflows that previously resisted automation. (Deloitte Insights) Another Deloitte analysis highlights the potential for agentic AI to increase productivity by automating multi-step tasks across business functions — even as adoption remains in the early stages for many organizations. (Deloitte.com)

Additionally, independent research and benchmarking efforts are emerging to better evaluate agent capabilities in real-world tasks and enterprise-relevant scenarios. Recent work on enterprise-focused benchmark processes billions of tokens to assess agent performance, reflecting the growing emphasis on *long-horizon, decision-oriented tasks* rather than simple completion accuracy. (arxiv.org)

2028-2030: Agent Scaling, Specialization and Regulatory Pressure

As agentic AI systems evolve beyond generic chatbots into **specialized expert agents tailored for professional domains**, companies are building models and platforms designed to meet the specific needs of regulated industries. For example, **Harvey AI** has positioned itself as a generative AI platform specifically for legal professionals, augmenting legal research, contract analysis, litigation support, and other practice-specific tasks for large law firms and corporate legal teams; it has entered global partnerships with firms like CMS and is expanding internationally with strategic agreements and bespoke deployments across multiple jurisdictions. (cms.law)

In enterprise software, startups such as **Contextual AI** focus on **specialized Retrieval-Augmented Generation (RAG) agents** for sectors including technology, banking, finance, and media, highlighting a clear move toward domain-specific agent tooling rather than one-size-fits-all models. (Wikipedia) Meanwhile, companies like **Cohere** have publicly shifted their AI strategy toward **enterprise-focused model deployments**, prioritizing secure, customizable models for regulated industries such as finance and healthcare and offering knowledge worker applications like its "North" tool in collaboration with enterprise customers. (Reuters)

Other specialist vendors are emerging in adjacent professional spaces as well—legal tech company **Eudia** has raised significant capital to develop AI tools for corporate legal departments and alternative legal service operations, emphasizing compliance and workflow automation tailored to legal work. (Wikipedia) In vertical sectors such as real estate and healthcare, enterprises like **EliseAI** are deploying AI agents that automate customer communications and administrative workflows specific to housing management and outpatient medical practice needs. (Wikipedia)

Concurrently, **regulation and compliance regimes are beginning to shape how these specialized AI systems are developed and deployed**. The European Union's **Artificial Intelligence Act (AI Act)** represents the first comprehensive legal framework governing AI, imposing risk-based requirements on developers and deployers of AI systems, including enhanced obligations for transparency, accountability, and safety in high-impact applications—a framework expected to materially influence enterprise risk management and product design decisions for AI providers operating in or targeting the EU market. (artificialintelligenceact.eu) National authorities and the newly established European AI Office are taking steps toward enforcement, supervising compliance and preparing guidance for obligations ranging from conformity assessments to market surveillance of advanced AI systems. (digital-strategy.ec.europa.eu) Voluntary EU codes of practice and draft guidelines on general-purpose AI further illustrate how regulatory frameworks are already reshaping expectations for transparency and compliance ahead of full enforcement timelines. (APnews)

Together, these developments show a clear industry shift: **domain-specific, expert AI agents are emerging as the primary commercial trajectories** for enterprise AI, while regulatory bodies like those implementing the EU AI Act are moving from design into **practical enforcement and compliance requirements that materially affect how these systems are built and used**.

2031-2035: Physical Autonomy, Automation, Societal Integration

Advances in **robotics combined with multimodal world models and long-horizon planning** are creating the foundation for scalable real-world automation across industries such as warehouses, logistics, and even specialized domains like lab automation. Research into *vision-language-action models*—which integrate vision, language, and action planning into a unified framework for robot control—illustrates how AI is being shaped to reason about physical tasks end-to-end rather than merely respond to isolated inputs, a necessary capability for robots that must plan and execute multi-step instructions in variable environments. These embodied models allow robots to translate sensory data into sequences of actionable commands, a prerequisite for long-horizon physical autonomy. (Wikipedia)

Companies and research labs are already demonstrating how these breakthroughs translate into real applications. For example, **Covariant** has developed the *Covariant Brain* and its *RFM-1 robotics foundation model* to help warehouse robots reason about object manipulation and order sortation at scale, enabling automation in logistics operations previously dominated by manual labor. (Wikipedia) In parallel, humanoid robotics efforts such as **1X's "Neo"** android are pushing toward safe, stable robot partners that could assist humans in logistics, retail, and other labor-intensive settings outside the lab. (LinkedIn) These technologies, when paired with sophisticated world models and planning systems, point toward a future where robots routinely handle complex tasks with minimal human intervention.

As physical agents become more capable, AI is evolving into a core infrastructure **layer** underpinning large parts of the economy. The **2025 Stanford HAI AI Index Report** highlights how AI adoption has accelerated across organizations, with majority use now reported across business functions and infrastructure costs plummeting due to efficiency gains in both software and hardware stacks. This trend toward AI ubiquity means the technology is no longer an add-on but a backbone for capabilities such as *OS-level assistants, industry-specific autonomous agents, and self-optimizing supply chains.* (LinkedIn) In supply chain and logistics, academic analysis underscores AI's potential to dramatically improve value chain operations spanning delivery, warehousing, and fulfillment by leveraging predictive analytics, automation, and optimization techniques that enhance efficiency and responsiveness. (gsb.stanford.edu)

These shifts are yielding **noticeable economic and social impacts**. As AI tools automate more routine cognitive and physical work, early productivity gains are already surfacing in diverse functions like service operations and supply chain management, with Stanford's report documenting measurable cost savings and revenue growth tied to AI deployment across sectors. (hai.stanford.edu) However, productivity increases are not uniform and are concentrated where automation can complement or replace labor-intensive work, reshaping the distribution of value toward firms that control AI platforms and infrastructure, as well as toward regions and sectors with favorable adoption dynamics. (LinkedIn)

The **"why"** behind this rapid evolution is the powerful positive feedback loop emerging from continued **compute and algorithmic progress, combined with task data collected from deployed agents**. As models improve and are embedded in real systems, they generate data and insights that feed back into better training, planning, and control algorithms—a dynamic akin to *accelerating returns* seen in scaling studies where increasing computational investment and richer data lead to systematically better performance. This phenomenon has been documented in work on embodied and multimodal AI systems that integrate perception and planning to improve autonomy in complex environments. (arxiv.org)

To know when this transformation has truly arrived, two **markers to watch** include:

- The emergence of **reliable, general-purpose physical agents** that can autonomously accomplish real-world tasks involving uncertainty and multi-step decision making without constant human oversight (a key test of embodied intelligence).
- A situation where **substantial fractions of industry workflows—such as R&D, logistics, and customer service—are executed end-to-end with minimal human intervention**, signaling that AI is not just a productivity booster but the operational core of these systems.

The key is that AI isn't some mysterious intelligence—it's a powerful tool that's really good at finding patterns and making predictions, but it's still just software created by people, with all the strengths and flaws that come with that creation. With this in mind - let's dive in...

One
Understanding AI Through the Familiar
How Machines Learn Like We Do

AI is like teaching a computer to recognize patterns the way you do. When you see a dog, you instantly know it's a dog because you've seen many dogs before. AI works similarly—it learns from lots of examples.

When we try to understand artificial intelligence, we often get lost in technical jargon, complex mathematics, and abstract concepts that seem far removed from everyday life. But the truth is, AI works in ways that are surprisingly similar to how you already learn and make sense of the world around you. By exploring this connection between human learning and machine learning, we can demystify AI and see it for what it really is: a technology that mirrors some of the most fundamental aspects of human cognition.

The Pattern Recognition We Do Every Day

Let's start with something you do effortlessly hundreds of times each day: recognizing things. Right now, as you read these words, you're recognizing letters, forming them into words, understanding their meanings, and combining those meanings into larger ideas. You didn't think about how to do any of that—it just happened. This automatic recognition is at the heart of both human intelligence and artificial intelligence.

Consider what happens when you walk down a street in your neighborhood. You see a four-legged animal approaching, and within a fraction of a second, you know it's a dog. You don't need to consciously think through a checklist: "Does it have fur? Check. Does it have four legs? Check. Does it have a tail? Check." The recognition is instantaneous and intuitive. Even more remarkably, you can recognize that it's a dog whether it's a tiny Chihuahua or a massive Great Dane, whether it's standing still or running, whether you see it from the front, side, or back.

This is pattern recognition, and it's one of the most fundamental capabilities of human intelligence. We're constantly matching what we see, hear, and experience against patterns we've learned throughout our lives. When you hear someone's voice on the phone, you instantly know who it is. When you smell coffee brewing, you recognize that smell immediately. When you touch something soft and fuzzy, you can guess what kind of texture it has. All of these are examples of pattern recognition happening automatically in your brain.

Now here's the fascinating part: this is essentially what AI does too. When we say AI "learns," we mean it develops the ability to recognize patterns in data, just like you've developed the ability to recognize patterns in your sensory experiences. The main difference is that you learned to recognize dogs through real-world experiences over many years, while AI learns to recognize dogs by processing thousands or millions of images in a matter of hours or days.

How You Actually Learned to Recognize a Dog

To understand how AI learns, it helps to think about how you learned to recognize things in the first place. You weren't born knowing what a dog was. As a baby or young child, someone probably pointed at a dog and said "dog" or "puppy." Maybe it was your family's pet, or a dog you saw at a park, or a picture in a children's book. That was your first example.

But one example isn't enough to truly learn what a dog is. If the first dog you ever saw was a Golden Retriever, you might initially think that "dog" means "big yellow fluffy animal." Then you saw another dog—maybe a small black Poodle—, and someone told you that it was also a dog. Your brain started adjusting its understanding: dogs can be different sizes and colors. Then you saw a Dachshund with its long body and short legs, and your concept of "dog" expanded again to include different body shapes.

Over time, you saw dozens, then hundreds, then thousands of different dogs. Some had floppy ears, others had pointy ears. Some had long fur, others had short fur, and some had barely any fur at all. They came in every color and size imaginable. But through all these examples, your brain was extracting something essential—the underlying pattern that makes a dog a dog, despite all the superficial differences.

Your brain was also learning what a dog is not. When you saw a cat, you learned that even though cats have four legs and fur like dogs, they're different. Cats move differently, have different facial features, make different sounds, and have a different overall "feel" to them. When you saw a horse, you learned that being a four-legged animal with hair doesn't automatically make something a dog—size and proportions matter too. Through these contrasting examples, your understanding became more refined and accurate.

This learning process happened mostly unconsciously. You weren't aware that your brain was building a complex model of what "dog-ness" looks like. You just looked at lots of dogs, and gradually, the ability to recognize them became second nature. Today, you can spot a dog instantly, even in challenging conditions—in low light, from a distance, partially hidden behind a tree, or in a photo you've never seen before. Your brain has become an expert pattern recognition system for dogs.

How AI Learns the Same Way

Artificial intelligence, particularly the type called "machine learning," works in a remarkably similar way. Instead of a human brain learning from experiences, we have a computer program learning from data. But the fundamental process of learning from examples to recognize patterns is essentially the same.

Let's walk through how we would teach an AI system to recognize dogs, and you'll see the parallels to human learning. First, we would gather a large dataset of images—some containing dogs and some not. This dataset is the AI's version of all those real-world experiences you had as a child. Just as you need to see many different dogs to learn what dogs look like, the AI needs to see many different examples.

We might start with 10,000 images: 5,000 that contain dogs and 5,000 that don't. Each image is labeled—we tell the AI, “This one has a dog," or "This one doesn't have a dog." This is like when someone pointed at animals and told you "dog" or "cat" when you were learning. The AI can't learn without these labels initially, just like you needed someone to teach you the names of things.

Now comes the learning process. The AI system starts by making random guesses. It looks at the first image and might guess "dog" even though there's no dog in it. We tell it “Wrong," and the system adjusts its internal parameters slightly. It looks at the next image and guesses again. Wrong again? It adjusts further. Right this time? It notes what it did and tries to do more of that.

This might sound tedious, but remember: computers can process information incredibly quickly. The AI can look at all 10,000 images and make guesses on all of them, receive feedback on each one, and adjust itself accordingly—all in minutes or hours. It's like compressed learning, taking a process that took you years and condensing it into a much shorter timeframe.

As the AI processes more examples, something remarkable happens. It starts to get better at recognizing dogs. At first, it might only recognize obvious cases—clear photos of typical-looking dogs in standard positions. But as it sees more diverse examples, it learns to recognize dogs from different angles, in different lighting, partially obscured, or in unusual positions. It's building up the same kind of flexible, robust pattern recognition that you have.

The AI also learns from its mistakes, just like you did. If it keeps mistaking cats for dogs, it will gradually learn the differences between them. If it thinks a fox is a dog, it will adjust to distinguish between similar-looking animals. Through thousands of iterations of making predictions and getting feedback, the system becomes increasingly accurate.

The Hidden Patterns That Both Humans and AI Learn

Here's where it gets really interesting: neither you nor an AI system can easily explain exactly how you recognize a dog. If someone asked you to write down a precise set of rules that would let anyone identify a dog in any situation, you'd find it incredibly difficult. You might start with obvious things like "has four legs" and "has fur," but then you'd encounter exceptions and edge cases. What about a three-legged dog? What about hairless dogs? What about stuffed toy dogs or cartoon dogs?

The truth is, you recognize dogs through a complex combination of features that you can't fully articulate. It's something about the proportions of the body, the shape of the face, the way the eyes are positioned, the texture and movement of the creature, and countless other subtle cues that your brain processes unconsciously. You've internalized a rich, nuanced understanding of "dog-ness" that goes far beyond any simple checklist.

AI systems work the same way. After training, the AI doesn't have a simple list of rules like "if four legs and fur and wet nose, then dog." Instead, it has learned a complex pattern—a combination of visual features, spatial relationships, textures, and shapes that together indicate the presence of a dog. Like you, it would struggle to explain exactly how it knows a dog when it sees one. The knowledge is embedded in the system in a way that's difficult to extract and express in simple terms.

This is actually one of the challenges with modern AI. When an AI system makes a decision — like identifying a dog in an image — we can see that it's correct, but we often can't see exactly how it arrived at that conclusion. The system has learned patterns that work, but they are represented in a mathematically complex, not easily interpretable way. It's a bit like asking you to explain exactly which neurons in your brain fire in what sequence when you recognize a dog — the knowledge is there, and it works, but it's not stored in a form that's easy to articulate.

Beyond Dogs: The Universal Nature of Pattern Learning

The dog example is just one instance of a much broader principle. Everything you know how to recognize—faces, voices, emotions, words, objects, places—you learned through this same process of exposure to many examples. You can recognize your best friend's face even though every time you see them, the lighting is different, the angle is different, their expression is different, and they might look tired or have gotten a haircut. Your brain has learned the underlying pattern of their face that persists across all these variations.

AI can learn to recognize all these things too, using the same fundamental approach. Modern AI systems can recognize faces, often with accuracy that matches or exceeds human ability. They can identify emotions in facial expressions, recognize objects in images, understand spoken words, read handwritten text, and detect patterns in everything from medical images to financial data.

Consider speech recognition, like what happens when you talk to Siri, Alexa, or Google Assistant. You speak naturally, with your own accent, at your own pace, with background noise, and the AI understands your words. How? It learned from thousands of hours of recorded speech, with transcriptions showing what words were actually said. Through exposure to countless examples of how different people pronounce words in different contexts, the AI learned to recognize speech patterns just like you learned to understand spoken language as a child.

Or consider how Netflix recommends shows you might like, or how Amazon suggests products. These systems have learned patterns in viewing and purchasing behavior. They've seen millions of examples of what people watch or buy, and they've learned to recognize patterns like "people who liked Show A also tend to like Show B" or "people who bought this kind of product often buy that kind too." It's pattern recognition applied to behavior rather than images, but the underlying learning process is the same.

The Power of Examples Over Rules

This example-based learning approach represents a fundamental shift from how we traditionally programmed computers. In traditional programming, humans figure out the rules and explicitly tell the computer what to do in every situation. If you were writing a traditional computer program to sort mail, you might write rules like "if the ZIP code starts with 900-999, send it to California." You'd need to consider every possibility and write explicit instructions for each.

But with AI and machine learning, we don't write the rules. We just show the system lots of examples, and it figures out the patterns on its own. For recognizing dogs, this is vastly more practical than trying to write explicit rules. Imagine trying to write down every possible rule for identifying a dog—every possible shape, size, color, position, lighting condition, and viewing angle. It would be nearly impossible, and even if you could do it, the rules would be rigid and brittle, likely failing in many real-world situations.

Learning from examples is powerful because it's flexible and robust. Just as you can recognize a dog even in a photo taken from an angle and in lighting conditions you've never experienced before, a well-trained AI can generalize from its training examples to new situations. It doesn't need to have seen every possible dog in every possible situation—it learns the underlying patterns well enough to recognize new examples.

This is why AI has become so good at tasks that are easy for humans but were traditionally very hard for computers. Humans find it easy to recognize faces, understand speech, or identify objects because we're naturally good at learning from examples and recognizing patterns. Traditional programming struggled with these tasks because they're almost impossible to reduce to explicit rules. But machine learning excels at them because it learns the same way we do—from lots and lots of examples.

The Importance of Good Examples

Just as the quality and diversity of your childhood experiences affected what you learned, the quality and diversity of training data affect what AI learns. If you had only ever seen Golden Retrievers as a child, you might struggle to recognize other breeds as dogs. Similarly, if an AI is trained mostly on images of one type of dog, it might not recognize other types as well.

This is why the data used to train AI systems is so important. If you train an AI to recognize faces using photos of mostly young people, it might not perform as well on faces of elderly people. If you train a speech recognition system mostly on speakers with American accents, it might struggle with British or Australian accents. The AI learns what it's shown, and its knowledge reflects the examples it has seen.

This also means AI can learn biases present in its training data. If you grew up in a place where everyone spoke negatively about a particular group of people, you might internalize those biases even though you never explicitly decided to be biased. AI systems can have the same problem. If they're trained on data that reflects human biases—and most real-world data does—then the AI can learn and perpetuate those biases. This is one of the major challenges in developing fair and equitable AI systems.

The good news is that just as people can learn to overcome biases by exposing themselves to more diverse experiences and perspectives, AI systems can be improved by training them on more diverse and representative data. Researchers are actively working on techniques to make AI systems fairer and more robust by carefully curating training data and developing methods to detect and correct learned biases.

Multiple Layers of Pattern Recognition

Your brain doesn't recognize a dog all at once—it builds up the recognition through multiple stages of processing. Your eyes detect basic features like edges and colors. Those basic features are combined into slightly more complex patterns like shapes and textures. Those are combined into parts of objects like ears, noses, and legs. Finally, those parts are combined into the recognition of "dog." This happens so fast and automatically that you're not aware of the stages, but they're there.

Many modern AI systems, particularly those called "deep learning" or "neural networks," work the same way. They process information through multiple layers, with each layer learning to recognize increasingly complex patterns. The first layer might learn to recognize simple features like edges and colors in an image. The second layer combines those simple features to recognize textures and basic shapes. The third layer might recognize parts like ears or noses. The final layer combines all this information to make the decision: "dog" or "not dog."

This layered approach is why these systems are called "deep" learning—they have multiple layers of pattern recognition, each building on the previous one. It's also why they can be so powerful. Just as your brain's multi-stage processing lets you recognize incredibly complex patterns in the world, deep learning systems can recognize complex patterns in data.

Learning Takes Time and Repetition

You didn't learn to recognize dogs from seeing just one or two examples. It took many exposures, spread over time, with feedback and correction. The same is true for AI. Training an AI system requires many examples —thousands or millions, depending on the complexity of what it's learning. And the training process involves many iterations, where the system gradually improves through repeated exposure to examples and feedback.

This is actually one of the reasons AI has become so powerful only recently. For machine learning to work well, you need large amounts of data and substantial computing power to process all that data through many iterations of learning. As our digital world has generated more and more data—billions of images on the internet, millions of hours of video, vast amounts of text—and as computers have become more powerful, it's become possible to train AI systems on a scale that wasn't feasible before.

Think about all the photos taken every day and uploaded to the internet, all the videos posted, all the text written. This massive amount of data represents opportunities for AI to learn patterns. An AI system learning to recognize cats can train on millions of cat photos. An AI learning to translate languages can train on billions of sentences that have been translated by humans. The abundance of data in our digital age has been crucial to the success of modern AI.

The Limits of Learning from Examples

Just as human learning from examples has limitations, so does AI learning. You might be great at recognizing dogs because you've seen thousands of them, but if you suddenly encounter an animal you've never seen before—say, a platypus—you might struggle to identify it or even believe it's real. You don't have the right pattern stored in your brain because you've never been exposed to examples.

AI has the same limitations. If an AI system has been trained to recognize dogs but never seen a wolf, it might misclassify a wolf as a dog because the patterns are similar. Or if it's trained on photos of animals in natural settings, it might struggle with animals in unusual contexts—like a dog wearing clothes or standing on its hind legs. It can only recognize patterns it has learned from its training data.

This is why AI systems can sometimes fail in surprising ways. They might be superhuman at tasks they've been specifically trained on, but completely helpless when faced with something even slightly outside their training experience. A system that's excellent at recognizing dogs in photos might fail completely if you show it a cartoon dog or a sculpture of a dog, because those weren't in its training data and represent different kinds of patterns.

Humans are generally better at transferring knowledge from one domain to another. If you've never seen a platypus before, but I describe it to you as "a mammal with a duck bill and beaver tail that lays eggs," you can imagine what to look for and would probably recognize one if you saw it. Most current AI systems can't do this kind of flexible reasoning based on descriptions—they need to learn from direct examples.

The Social Aspect of Learning

When you learned to recognize dogs, you didn't do it in isolation. Other people helped you—they pointed at dogs, said the word "dog," corrected you when you got it wrong, and confirmed when you got it right. Human learning is fundamentally social. We learn from each other, and much of what we know comes from other people teaching us, either explicitly or through observation.

AI learning has a similar social component, though it's less obvious. The labels on training data—the information saying "this image contains a dog" or "this image doesn't"—represent human knowledge. People had to look at those images and label them, transferring their knowledge to the AI. In a sense, when you use an AI system that recognizes dogs, you're benefiting from the collective knowledge of all the people who labeled the training images, just as you benefit from the people who taught you.

There are even AI systems that learn from human feedback in more interactive ways. For example, some systems learn by having humans rate their outputs—saying which responses are good and which are bad. This is similar to how you learned things by getting positive feedback when you were right and corrective feedback when you were wrong. The AI adjusts its behavior based on this feedback, learning to do more of what humans approve of and less of what they don't.

The Joy and Ease of Recognition

One of the most remarkable things about pattern recognition, whether in humans or AI, is how effortless it seems once learned. You don't struggle to recognize a dog when you see one—the recognition just happens, instantly and automatically. You don't have to think about it or work through it step by step. The same is true for a well-trained AI system. Once trained, recognition is fast and automatic.

But that ease is deceptive. Behind that instant recognition lies thousands, or even millions, of learning experiences, countless adjustments and refinements, and complex internal processing that you're not aware of. The effortlessness you experience is actually the end result of an elaborate learning process and sophisticated neural machinery working seamlessly in the background.

This is true for AI as well. An AI system might recognize a dog in an image in milliseconds, making it seem simple. But that instant recognition is the result of processing millions of training images through billions of mathematical operations to learn the right patterns. The simplicity is in the use, not in what makes it work.

Looking at Your Own Intelligence Differently

Understanding that AI learns through examples helps us appreciate something profound about our own intelligence. Much of what you know—maybe most of what you know—you learned not through explicit instruction but through exposure to examples and pattern recognition. You learned your native language not by studying grammar rules but by hearing millions of sentences. You learned to navigate social situations not from a rulebook but from observing thousands of interactions and learning what works.

In a way, you are a pattern recognition machine, exquisitely tuned by evolution and shaped by your experiences. The fact that AI can learn in similar ways isn't diminishing to human intelligence—rather, it reveals something impressive about the learning strategies that humans use. Pattern recognition from examples is a powerful way to acquire knowledge, powerful enough that it works whether implemented in biological neurons or silicon circuits.

The Familiar Made Strange

So when we say AI is like teaching a computer to recognize patterns the way you do, we're not just using a metaphor to make AI seem more understandable. We're describing a deep similarity in how learning actually works. Both you and AI systems:

- Learn from examples rather than explicit rules
- Need many diverse examples to learn effectively
- Extract underlying patterns that generalize to new situations
- Build up complex recognition through multiple layers of simpler patterns
- Improve with practice and feedback
- Can learn biases from their training experiences
- Make recognition seem effortless once learned
- Struggle with things outside their experience

The main differences are in scale, speed, and flexibility. AI can process far more examples much faster than a human, but humans are much better at transferring knowledge across domains and learning from very few examples when needed. Humans can understand abstract explanations and analogies, while most current AI needs direct examples. And human learning is deeply integrated with consciousness, emotion, and understanding in ways that AI isn't.

But the fundamental process—learning to recognize patterns through exposure to examples—is remarkably similar. This means that your own experience as a learner gives you genuine insight into how AI works. When you wonder how an AI could possibly recognize something as varied and complex as "dog" across countless different situations, you can remember that you do exactly that, and you learned the same way the AI did: through lots and lots of examples over time.

Conclusion: The Familiar Becomes the Technological

Understanding AI through this lens of familiar learning processes makes it less mysterious and more accessible. AI isn't some alien intelligence working in incomprehensible ways. It's technology that leverages the same powerful learning strategy that made you the intelligent, capable pattern recognizer you are today.

When you use an AI-powered app that recognizes your face to unlock your phone, it's using the same basic learning approach that lets your brain recognize your friend's face in a crowd. When you talk to a voice assistant that understands your words, it learns from examples just like you learned to understand speech. When an AI recommends a movie you end up loving, it recognizes a pattern in your preferences using the same kind of pattern-matching that happens in your brain when you recognize things you like.

This doesn't mean AI and human intelligence are identical—they're not. But it does mean that the core learning mechanism of much modern AI is grounded in something deeply familiar: the power of learning from examples to recognize patterns. And that's something every person understands intuitively, even if they've never thought about it explicitly.

The next time you instantly recognize something—a face, a voice, a place, an object—you can appreciate that you're doing something remarkably sophisticated, something that took years of learning from countless examples. And you can understand that when AI does something similar, it's not magic or mystery. It's pattern recognition, learned from examples, just like what you do every day without even thinking about it. The familiar has become technological, and understanding the familiar reveals the foundation of AI.

Two
AI Is Not Magic, It's Math
Understanding the Numbers Behind the Intelligence

At its core, AI is really sophisticated pattern-matching using statistics and lots of calculations. It's finding connections in huge amounts of data that would take humans forever to spot.

When you first encounter artificial intelligence that can write poetry, recognize your face, or beat world champions at complex games, it can feel like magic. How can a machine possibly do these things that seem to require creativity, understanding, and intelligence? The answer might surprise you in its simplicity: AI doesn't work through any mysterious force or consciousness. At its foundation, AI is mathematics—specifically, it's enormous amounts of arithmetic being performed very, very quickly to find patterns in data.

This might seem disappointing at first. We want AI to be mysterious and profound, not just calculations. But actually, the fact that math alone can produce such impressive results is its own kind of wonder. Let's explore exactly how numbers, statistics, and calculations create what appears to be intelligence.

What We Mean by "Just Math"

When we say AI is "just math," we're being literal. Every single thing an AI does—every word it writes, every image it recognizes, every decision it makes—is the result of mathematical operations. Addition, subtraction, multiplication, and division, performed millions or billions of times, following specific mathematical formulas. There's no secret sauce, no mysterious element that can't be written down as an equation.

Think about a calculator for a moment. When you type "2 + 2" into a calculator, it doesn't "understand" addition in any meaningful sense. It follows a set of electronic operations that implement the mathematical rules of addition, and it displays "4." The calculator is performing math, and that's all it's doing. AI is similar, just vastly more complex. Instead of one simple calculation, AI performs astronomical numbers of calculations, and instead of adding two numbers, it processes massive amounts of data through intricate mathematical formulas. But fundamentally, it's still just math.

Let's make this concrete. Imagine you have a picture of a dog, and you want an AI to recognize that it's a dog. That image is stored on a computer as numbers—millions of them. Each tiny pixel in the image has a numeric value representing its color. A typical photo might be 1000 pixels wide and 1000 pixels tall, giving you a million pixels. Each pixel has three numbers representing how much red, green, and blue it contains. So your single photo is actually three million numbers.

The AI takes those three million numbers and processes them through a series of mathematical operations. It multiplies these numbers by other numbers (called "weights" or "parameters"), adds the results together, applies some mathematical functions to those sums, and repeats this process through multiple layers of calculations. After millions or billions of individual arithmetic operations, the system produces a final set of numbers that represents its conclusion: the probability that this image contains a dog, a cat, a car, or any number of other things.

That's it. That's the whole process. Numbers go in, mathematical operations happen, and numbers come out. No magic, no consciousness, no understanding—just calculations.

The Power of Very Simple Math Done Many Times

Here's something that seems almost magical but is actually pure mathematics: if you do simple operations enough times, in the right combinations, you can approximate incredibly complex functions. This is a fundamental principle in mathematics, and it's the key to understanding how AI works.

Let me give you an analogy. Imagine you're trying to draw a perfect circle, but you can only draw straight lines. This seems impossible—how can straight lines make a curve? But here's the trick: if you draw many very short straight-line segments, each at a slightly different angle, you can approximate a circle. The more line segments you use, the smoother your circle becomes. With enough tiny segments, your "circle" becomes indistinguishable from a perfect mathematical circle.

AI works on a similar principle. The mathematical operations AI uses are relatively simple—mostly multiplication, addition, and a few other basic functions. But by chaining together millions or billions of these simple operations in clever ways, the system can approximate extremely complex relationships between inputs and outputs. It can learn to map three million numbers representing an image to the concept "dog." It can learn to map a sequence of words to an appropriate next word. It can learn to map a chess board position to the best next move.

Each individual calculation is trivial. But the collective effect of millions of calculations, with the right numbers plugged in, can produce remarkably sophisticated behavior.

Statistics: Finding Patterns in Chaos

At the heart of AI is statistics, which is the branch of mathematics that deals with collecting, analyzing, and interpreting data. Statistics gives us tools for finding patterns and making predictions based on those patterns. And that's exactly what AI is doing—finding statistical patterns in data.

Let's understand this with a simple example. Imagine you're trying to predict whether it will rain tomorrow. You could look at today's weather and make a guess. But a better approach would be to look at historical data. You gather information about the weather for the past 1,000 days: temperature, humidity, air pressure, cloud cover, and whether it rained the next day. Now you can do statistical analysis on this data.

You might discover patterns: when humidity is above 80% and air pressure is dropping, it rains the next day 75% of the time. When humidity is low and pressure is rising, it rains only 5% of the time. These are statistical patterns—relationships between variables that hold true more often than not, but not always.

With this statistical knowledge, you can make predictions. Tomorrow's weather forecast becomes a mathematical problem: given today's humidity, temperature, and pressure readings, what do the historical patterns suggest about tomorrow's rain probability? You're not magically knowing the future—you're using math to find patterns in past data and extrapolating those patterns forward.

AI does exactly this, but with far more variables and far more data. When an AI learns to recognize dogs in images, it's finding statistical patterns in the millions of pixels that make up images of dogs. It discovers things like: when certain pixel patterns appear in certain arrangements, there's a high probability that the image contains a dog. It's not "understanding" what a dog is in any philosophical sense—it's finding mathematical relationships between pixel values and the label "dog."

Numbers Representing Everything

For AI to work its mathematical magic, everything needs to be converted into numbers. This might seem limiting, but it's actually incredibly powerful because almost anything can be represented numerically.

We already mentioned that images are numbers—pixel values representing colors. But what about text? How do you turn words into numbers? There are many approaches, but here's a simple one: you could assign each word a number. "The" might be 1, "cat" might be 2, "sat" might be 3, and so on. Then the sentence "the cat sat" becomes the sequence of numbers "1 2 3." More sophisticated approaches encode not just which word it is, but information about its meaning, its grammatical role, and its relationships to other words—all as numbers.

Sounds can be represented as numbers, too. A sound wave is really just air pressure changing over time. If you measure that pressure thousands of times per second and record each measurement as a number, you've converted sound into numbers. That's what happens when you record audio digitally—the computer is storing a long list of numbers representing the amplitude of the sound wave at each moment.

Even abstract concepts can be turned into numbers. If you want to represent a person's preference for different types of movies, you could create a list of numbers: 8 out of 10 for action movies, 3 out of 10 for horror, 7 out of 10 for comedy, and so on. Their preferences are now a mathematical vector—a list of numbers that can be processed mathematically.

Once everything is represented as numbers, AI can apply mathematics to find patterns and make predictions. This is why AI has been successfully applied to so many different domains. Whether it's images, text, sound, machine sensor data, financial records, or medical information, if it can be turned into numbers, AI can analyze it mathematically.

The Core Mathematical Operation: Multiplication and Addition

Let's get specific about what calculations AI actually does. At the most basic level, the fundamental operation is remarkably simple: multiply some numbers together, add up the results, and possibly apply a simple function to the sum.

Imagine you're trying to decide whether to take an umbrella today. You might consider several factors: the humidity (let's say 70%), the cloud cover (80%), and what the weather forecast says (60% chance of rain).

Intuitively, you give different weights to these factors. Maybe you trust the weather forecast most, so it counts for 50% of your decision. Cloud cover counts for 30%, and humidity for 20%.

Your decision process could be mathematical:

- Weather forecast (0.6) × importance (0.5) = 0.30
- Cloud cover (0.8) × importance (0.3) = 0.24
- Humidity (0.7) × importance (0.2) = 0.14
- Total = 0.30 + 0.24 + 0.14 = 0.68

Since 0.68 is above 0.5, you take the umbrella. You've just performed a weighted sum—you multiplied each input by a weight representing its importance, added up the results, and used that to make a decision.

This exact type of calculation is the building block of AI. An AI system contains millions or billions of these weights. When it processes data, it's constantly performing these weighted sums. For recognizing a dog in an image, some pixels might have high weights (because they're in areas where dog features typically appear) and others might have low weights. The system multiplies each pixel value by its weight, adds them all up, and uses the result to help decide whether there's a dog in the image.

The magical part—and this is where the "intelligence" emerges—is that the system learns what weights to use through exposure to examples. Initially, the weights are random, and the system's predictions are terrible. But through a mathematical process called optimization, the weights are gradually adjusted to improve the system's accuracy. After processing millions of examples and adjusting the weights millions of times, the system ends up with a set of weights that encode useful patterns for recognizing dogs.

Learning as Mathematical Optimization

The learning process in AI is itself a mathematical procedure. It's called "optimization," and it's a technique for finding the best values for a set of parameters to minimize some error or maximize some objective.

Here's a simple analogy. Imagine you're trying to adjust the temperature of your shower to exactly 100 degrees Fahrenheit. You turn the hot water knob and measure the temperature—it's 80 degrees, too cold. So you turn the hot water up a bit. Now it's 110 degrees, too hot. You adjust down slightly. You keep making adjustments, each time measuring the temperature and moving the knob in the direction that gets you closer to your target. Eventually, you find the right position for the knob that gives you 100 degrees.

This is optimization. You had an error (the difference between the current temperature and your target), and you iteratively adjusted a parameter (the knob position) to reduce that error. The process is mathematical: measure the error, determine the direction to adjust the parameter, make the adjustment, and repeat.

AI learning works the same way, just with millions of parameters instead of one knob. The system makes a prediction (like identifying what's in an image), compares it to the correct answer, calculates the error, and then adjusts all its weights slightly in directions that would reduce the error. It does this thousands or millions of times, processing lots of examples, and gradually the weights converge to values that make good predictions.

The mathematics for figuring out how to adjust the weights is called "gradient descent" or "backpropagation," and it uses calculus—the branch of mathematics dealing with rates of change. The key insight is that you can calculate mathematically how much each weight contributed to the error, and therefore how to adjust it to reduce the error. It's all equations and arithmetic, no magic required.

Why Massive Scale Matters

Here's where the "lots of calculations" part becomes crucial. The mathematics underlying AI isn't particularly complicated—it's operations you learned in high school algebra and calculus. But the scale is staggering.

A modern AI system might have billions of parameters (weights). Training such a system might involve processing millions or billions of examples. For each example, the system performs billions of mathematical operations. So the total number of calculations during training is astronomical—quintillions or more.

To put this in perspective, if you were doing these calculations by hand with a calculator, and you could complete one calculation per second, it would take you billions of years to train a single modern AI system. But computers can perform billions of calculations per second, especially using specialized chips called GPUs (Graphics Processing Units) that are designed for doing many calculations simultaneously. What would take a human billions of years takes a computer hours or days.

This massive scale is what makes AI practical. The mathematics has been understood for decades, but only recently have computers become powerful enough to actually perform the necessary calculations in reasonable time frames. The "intelligence" of AI emerges from the sheer scale of mathematical computation—billions of parameters, learned from millions of examples, through quintillions of calculations.

Statistics: Correlation and Prediction

Let's dig deeper into the statistical side. One of the fundamental concepts in statistics is correlation—when two things tend to occur together or move together. AI is essentially a machine for discovering correlations in data.

Suppose you're analyzing data about students' test scores and study hours. You might discover a correlation: students who study more hours tend to get higher scores. This correlation is expressed mathematically as a number between -1 and 1, where 1 means perfect positive correlation, -1 means perfect negative correlation, and 0 means no correlation.

With this correlation, you can make predictions. If a new student studies 10 hours for a test, you can use the mathematical relationship you discovered to predict their likely score. You're not certain—correlation doesn't mean one thing causes the other, and there's always variation—but you can make an informed statistical prediction.

AI does this at scale with thousands or millions of variables. When learning to recognize dogs in images, it's finding statistical patterns in the millions of pixels that make up images of dogs. It discovers things like: when certain pixel patterns appear in certain arrangements, there's a high probability that the image contains a dog. It's not "understanding" what a dog is in any philosophical sense — it's finding mathematical relationships between pixel values and the label "dog."

All of these correlations are discovered through mathematical analysis of data. The system looks at the numbers, calculates statistical relationships between different variables, and encodes those relationships in its parameters. Then, when it encounters new data, it uses those learned correlations to make predictions.

Probability: Dealing with Uncertainty

Another crucial branch of mathematics in AI is probability theory—the mathematics of uncertainty. Real-world predictions are almost never certain. There's always variability, noise, and factors we don't know about.

AI systems typically don't output definitive answers; they output probabilities. When an image recognition system looks at a photo, it doesn't just say "dog" or "not dog." Instead, it calculates probabilities: 95% probability it's a dog, 3% probability it's a wolf, 1% probability it's a fox, 1% probability it's something else.

These probabilities come from the mathematical operations inside the system. The final layers of calculation typically include a mathematical function that converts the system's internal numbers into probabilities that sum to 100%. This function ensures the outputs can be interpreted as legitimate probability estimates.

Why probabilities instead of certainties? Because the system has learned that the world is uncertain. In its training data, similar-looking images sometimes had different labels. The system learned that when it sees certain patterns, there's a 95% chance of dogs, but occasionally those patterns appear with other animals too. The mathematical framework of probability lets the system express this uncertainty numerically.

This is actually more honest than absolute declarations. When you recognize a dog, you're also working with probabilities in your brain—you're just not consciously aware of them. If you see a blurry shape in the distance with four legs, you might be 70% sure it's a dog, 20% sure it's a different animal, and 10% unsure. AI makes these probability estimates explicit and numerical.

Matrix Mathematics: Processing Many Numbers Simultaneously

One reason AI can be so powerful is that it processes large amounts of data simultaneously using matrix mathematics. A matrix is just a rectangular grid of numbers, and there are mathematical rules for manipulating matrices efficiently.

Remember our image with three-million-pixel values? In AI systems, these aren't processed one at a time. Instead, they're organized into matrices and processed all at once using matrix operations. Modern computer chips can perform matrix multiplication extremely quickly—billions of matrix operations per second.

This parallel processing is crucial for AI's speed and capabilities. Instead of looking at each pixel individually, the system can look at entire regions of the image simultaneously. It can apply mathematical transformations to thousands or millions of numbers in one operation, extracting patterns at multiple scales at once.

The mathematics of matrices has been studied for centuries and is very well understood. Linear algebra—the branch of mathematics dealing with matrices and vectors—provides the foundation for much of modern AI. The "deep learning" revolution that has made AI so powerful in recent years is largely about figuring out how to cleverly arrange matrix operations to extract increasingly complex patterns from data.

Functions: Mapping Inputs to Outputs

Mathematically, what AI is doing is learning a function—a mathematical relationship that maps inputs to outputs. When you learned functions in school, you might have seen things like $f(x) = 2x + 3$. This function takes an input (x), performs some operations (multiply by 2, add 3), and produces an output.

AI is learning vastly more complicated functions, but the concept is the same. An image recognition AI is learning a function that takes three million numbers (the pixels) as input and produces probabilities for different objects as output. A language AI is learning a function that takes a sequence of words as input and produces the next word as output.

These functions are incredibly complex—they can't be written down as simple equations like $f(x) = 2x + 3$. They involve millions of parameters and nested layers of operations. But they're still mathematical functions, following deterministic mathematical rules. Given the same input, they always produce the same output, because the calculations are always the same.

The "learning" process is finding the right function—or more precisely, finding the right parameters for a very flexible template function. The template function structure is designed by AI researchers and engineers. It specifies the types of mathematical operations to perform and the order in which to perform them. But the specific numbers (parameters) that make the function work well are learned from data through the optimization process we discussed earlier.

Why This Feels Like More Than Math

Given that AI is "just math," why does it sometimes feel like more? Why does it seem intelligent, creative, or understanding? There are several reasons:

First, the scale and complexity hide the underlying simplicity. When you see billions of parameters processing millions of data points through quintillions of calculations, it's hard to keep in mind that each individual step is just arithmetic. The forest obscures the trees.

Second, we anthropomorphize. We see behavior that resembles human intelligence, and we instinctively attribute human-like mental processes to it. When AI writes a poem, we imagine it "thinking" about metaphors and emotions. But it's actually calculating probabilities for what word is likely to come next, based on patterns it learned from millions of example texts.

Third, the emergent properties are genuinely surprising. When simple operations are combined at a massive scale in clever ways, the resulting capabilities can be genuinely unexpected. Researchers don't always know in advance what an AI system will be capable of once trained. The emergent behavior can appear creative or insightful, even though it arises from mechanical mathematical processes.

Fourth, we don't understand the patterns the AI has learned. The billions of parameters in a trained AI system encode patterns discovered in the data, but those patterns are represented as vast arrays of numbers that don't translate into concepts we can easily interpret. So the system appears to be working through some mysterious process, when actually it's just applying learned statistical relationships that happen to be too complex for humans to comprehend directly.

The Limits of "Just Math"

Understanding that AI is mathematics also helps us understand its limitations. Math is powerful, but it has constraints:

- **Math requires data.** Unlike humans, who can sometimes reason from principles or make logical deductions, AI systems learn from examples. If the data is limited, biased, or unrepresentative, the mathematical patterns the system learns will be flawed.
- **Math finds correlations, not causes.** Statistical methods can discover that two things tend to occur together, but they can't inherently distinguish whether one causes the other, both are caused by something else, or the relationship is coincidental. AI can learn that dark clouds correlate with rain, but it doesn't "understand" the causal mechanism of weather.
- **Math is brittle.** Mathematical functions work well in the domains where they were trained, but they can fail dramatically when applied to different contexts. An AI trained on normal photos might be confused by artistic images, because the mathematical patterns are different.
- **Math has no common sense.** Humans bring vast background knowledge to every situation. We implicitly understand physics, social dynamics, psychology, and countless other domains. AI systems only have the mathematical patterns they extracted from their specific training data. They lack the broad, flexible understanding that humans develop.
- **Math doesn't understand meaning.** When an AI processes the word "dog," it's manipulating a numerical representation. It has learned statistical patterns about how that representation relates to other representations, but there's no semantic understanding—no mental concept of dog-ness, no knowledge of what it's like to pet a dog or hear one bark.

These aren't criticisms of AI, just recognition of what mathematical approaches can and cannot do. Math is spectacularly good at finding patterns in data and using those patterns for prediction and classification. But it's not good at things like abstract reasoning, causal understanding, generalization beyond training data, or anything requiring genuine understanding rather than pattern matching.

Different Math for Different Tasks

Not all AI uses the same mathematics. Different types of tasks call for different mathematical approaches:

- **Neural networks** use the layered weighted-sum approach we've discussed, inspired loosely by how neurons work in brains. They're good for perception tasks like recognizing images or understanding speech.
- **Decision trees** use branching logic that can be represented mathematically: if variable X is above threshold T, take the left branch, otherwise take the right branch. They're good for tasks where decisions follow hierarchical rules.
- **Bayesian methods** use probability theory to update beliefs based on evidence. They're good when you need to incorporate prior knowledge and quantify uncertainty carefully.
- **Reinforcement learning** uses mathematical optimization to learn strategies through trial and error, maximizing rewards over time. It's good for tasks like game playing or robot control.

But all of these are mathematical frameworks. They use different equations and different types of calculations, but they're all processing numbers according to mathematical rules to find patterns and make predictions.

The Computer's Role: Speed and Precision

It's worth emphasizing what computers bring to the table: speed and precision in calculation. Humans are terrible at performing millions of calculations accurately. We make arithmetic errors, we get tired, and we can't hold thousands of numbers in our heads simultaneously.

Computers excel at exactly what we're bad at. They can perform billions of calculations per second without getting tired or making mistakes (assuming the hardware works correctly). They can hold billions of numbers in memory and access them instantly. They never get bored with repetitive calculations.

This is why AI is implemented on computers rather than having humans calculate everything by hand. The mathematics would work the same way in principle if humans did all the calculations—it would just take billions of years. Computers make it practical by executing the mathematics at superhuman speed.

But the computer isn't adding anything magical. It's just very quickly following mathematical instructions. The intelligence isn't in the computer hardware—it's in the mathematics that the hardware is executing.

Debugging AI: When the Math Goes Wrong

The fact that AI is mathematics means that when it fails, we can analyze why mathematically. When an AI makes a mistake, it's because the mathematical function it learned doesn't correctly map the input to the desired output in this case.

This might happen because:

- The training data didn't include enough examples of this type of situation
- The mathematical structure of the network isn't flexible enough to represent the true relationship
- The optimization process found a local minimum instead of the best solution
- There was noise or errors in the training data that led to learning wrong patterns

All of these are mathematical issues that can be analyzed and potentially corrected with mathematical techniques. This is very different from trying to "debug" a mind or consciousness—we're debugging an equation, essentially.

Engineers working on AI spend a lot of time looking at what mathematical operations the system is performing, what patterns it has learned (to the extent they can be visualized), and how to adjust the mathematical framework to improve performance. It's engineering and applied mathematics, not psychology or philosophy.

The Beauty of Mathematical Intelligence

There's something profound about the fact that mathematics alone can produce intelligent-seeming behavior. For centuries, people assumed that intelligence required something beyond the physical—a soul, consciousness, or some ineffable quality. The success of AI shows that many intelligent behaviors can emerge from purely mathematical processes.

This doesn't mean human intelligence is nothing but math, or that consciousness is an illusion. But it does show that the connection between mathematical pattern-processing and intelligent behavior is deeper than we might have thought.

It's similar to how mathematics describes physics. The motions of planets, the flow of water, the behavior of light—all of these can be precisely described by mathematical equations. Mathematics isn't just an approximate description; it seems to be the language in which physical laws are written. Similarly, mathematics might be the language of information processing and pattern recognition, whether implemented in silicon or neurons.

Conclusion: Demystifying Intelligence

When we say AI is "not magic, it's math," we're demystifying intelligence without diminishing it. Understanding that AI works through statistics and computation doesn't make it less impressive—if anything, it makes it more impressive that so much can be achieved through mathematical principles.

Every time an AI recognizes your face, understands your voice, or generates coherent text, it's performing millions or billions of mathematical calculations. Pixels are multiplied by weights, sums are calculated, probabilities are computed, and patterns learned from vast datasets are applied. No consciousness, no understanding, no magic—just numbers, equations, and lots and lots of calculations.

This mathematical foundation means AI is comprehensible. We can write down the equations. We can trace through the calculations (at least in principle, though there are too many to do manually). We can analyze what went wrong when it fails. We can improve it by changing the mathematics or providing more data.

It also means AI inherits both the power and limitations of mathematics. It can find patterns humans never would have spotted in vast datasets, processing information at scales beyond human capacity. But it can also fail in ways that seem absurd to humans, because it's following mathematical relationships that don't capture the full complexity or context of the real world.

Understanding AI as mathematics helps us use it appropriately. We can appreciate its strengths—processing vast amounts of data, finding subtle correlations, and making consistent predictions at scale. And we can respect its limitations—lack of true understanding, dependence on training data, brittleness outside its training domain.

The next time you interact with AI, remember: you're not communing with an alien intelligence or tapping into some mysterious force. You're using the results of an enormous mathematical calculation, the product of billions of numbers being multiplied, added, and transformed according to patterns learned from data. It's mathematics at an impressive scale, applied cleverly to solve useful problems. Not magic—just math. Beautiful, powerful, practical math.

Three
AI Is Like Training, Not Programming
Understanding the Fundamental Shift in How Computers Learn

Traditional software follows explicit rules you write ("if this, then that"). AI learns from examples instead. You show it thousands of pictures of cats, and it figures out what makes something a cat.

When most people think about computers and software, they imagine programmers typing out instructions that tell the computer exactly what to do in every situation. This is programming, and it's been the dominant way of making computers useful for decades. But artificial intelligence represents a fundamentally different approach—one that's less like giving instructions and more like teaching a student. Understanding this difference is crucial to understanding what AI really is and why it's such a revolutionary technology.

The Traditional Way: Programming with Explicit Rules

Let's start by understanding what programming actually means. When you program a computer, you're writing explicit, step-by-step instructions that tell the computer exactly what to do in every possible situation. It's like writing an incredibly detailed recipe that accounts for every variation and possibility.

Imagine you're programming a simple calculator. You need to tell the computer: "When the user types two numbers and clicks the plus button, add those numbers together and display the result. When they click the minus button, subtract the second from the first. When they click multiply, multiply them," and so on. For every button, every operation, every possible input, you write explicit code saying exactly what should happen.

This approach works beautifully for tasks where the rules are clear, consistent, and can be completely specified. Math operations, database queries, sorting lists—these are all things where we can write down exact rules for every situation, and programming handles them perfectly.

Let's consider a more complex example: writing a program to determine if someone is eligible for a loan. The rules might be:

- If credit score is above 700 AND income is above $50,000, approve the loan
- If credit score is between 650-700 AND income is above $75,000, approve the loan
- If credit score is below 650, deny the loan
- If income is below $30,000, deny the loan
- And so on...

You, the programmer, think through all the rules, all the edge cases, all the combinations of conditions, and you write explicit code for each one. The computer will then follow your rules exactly, every single time, with perfect consistency. If the rules are good, the program works well. If you forgot a case or got a rule wrong, the program will fail.

This is the essence of traditional programming: humans figure out the rules, write them down as code, and the computer executes those rules mechanically. The intelligence—the decision-making about what rules to use—comes entirely from the human programmer.

Why Programming Doesn't Work for Everything

The programming approach is powerful, but it has a major limitation: many real-world problems don't have rules that can be easily written down. Consider the task of recognizing a cat in a photograph. How would you program that?

You might start with some rules:

- If the image has pointy ears, it might be a cat
- If it has whiskers, it might be a cat
- If it has four legs and fur, it might be a cat

But immediately, you run into problems. Dogs also have four legs and fur. Rabbits have pointy ears. Some cat photos show the cat from behind, where you can't see whiskers. Some photos are blurry, or the cat is partially hidden, or the lighting is strange. Some breeds of cats look very different from others—a hairless Sphynx cat looks nothing like a fluffy Persian.

You could try to write more elaborate rules: "If pointy ears AND whiskers AND the ears are positioned at a specific angle AND the face has a certain shape AND..." But the problem keeps growing. How do you specify "a certain shape" in code? How do you write a rule that works for all angles, all lighting conditions, all breeds, all poses?

The reality is that recognizing a cat is easy for a five-year-old child, but nearly impossible to capture in explicit programmed rules. The same is true for countless other tasks: recognizing faces, understanding speech, reading handwritten text, translating languages, playing strategic games, or writing coherent text. These tasks are easy for humans but extremely difficult to reduce to explicit rules that could be programmed.

This is where the fundamental limitation of traditional programming becomes clear: for many important problems, we humans don't actually know what rules we're using. We can recognize a cat instantly, but we can't explain the precise rules that let us do so. And if we can't explain the rules, we can't program them.

Enter the Training Approach: Learning from Examples

AI takes a completely different approach. Instead of trying to write down rules, we show the system lots of examples and let it figure out the patterns on its own. This is training, not programming.

Think about how you learned to recognize cats. Nobody sat you down and gave you a rulebook: "Cats have ears at a 60-degree angle, whiskers between 2-5 inches long, pupils that are vertical slits..." Instead, people pointed at cats and said "cat." They showed you picture books with cats. You saw cats in real life, on TV, and in various situations. After seeing dozens or hundreds of examples, you just understood what a cat was. You internalized the pattern of "cat-ness" without anyone ever explicitly teaching you the rules.

AI works the same way. Here's how we would train an AI system to recognize cats:

Step 1: Gather Examples. We collect thousands of images—let's say 50,000 photos. Half of them contain cats, half don't. Crucially, we label each image: "cat" or "not cat." These labels are teaching signals, like when someone pointed at an animal and told you "cat" when you were learning.

Step 2: Show Examples to the System. We show the AI system these images one by one (or in batches). At first, the system knows nothing. Its internal parameters are set randomly, so its guesses are random too. It looks at a cat photo and might guess "not cat." It looks at a photo of a car and might guess "cat." It's completely wrong most of the time because it hasn't learned anything yet.

Step 3: Provide Feedback. After each guess, we tell the system whether it was right or wrong. "No, that was a cat, you got it wrong." "Yes, that's not a cat, you got it right." This feedback is crucial—it's how the system learns.

Step 4: Let the System Adjust. This is where the "learning" happens. Based on the feedback, the system automatically adjusts its internal parameters slightly. If it incorrectly said "not cat" for a cat image, it adjusts itself in a direction that would make it more likely to say "cat" for similar images in the future. If it incorrectly said "cat" for a non-cat image, it adjusts to be less likely to say "cat" for similar images.

These adjustments are mathematical—the system is tweaking millions of numbers that control how it processes images. But you don't need to understand the math to grasp the concept: the system is modifying itself to perform better based on feedback.

Step 5: Repeat Thousands of Times. The system goes through all 50,000 images, making guesses and adjusting itself based on feedback. Then it goes through them all again. And again. And again. After dozens or hundreds of passes through the data, something remarkable happens: the system gets good at recognizing cats. It has learned patterns from examples, allowing it to correctly identify cats even in photos it's never seen before.

Notice what didn't happen: nobody wrote rules for what makes a cat. Nobody programmed the system with instructions about ears or whiskers. The programmer didn't need to understand what features distinguish cats from other animals. The system figured that out on its own by looking at examples.

Training vs. Programming: A Direct Comparison

Let's make the contrast crystal clear with a side-by-side comparison:

- **Traditional Programming:**
    - Programmer writes explicit rules
    - Rules cover every possible case
    - Computer follows rules exactly
    - Intelligence comes from the programmer
    - Works great when rules are knowable
    - Fails when rules are too complex to specify
    - Behavior is predictable and consistent

  - Easy to understand why decisions are made

- **AI Training:**
  - System is shown many examples
  - System finds patterns on its own
  - Computer learns general principles from examples
  - Intelligence emerges from the learning process
  - Works great even when rules are unknown
  - Requires lots of good example data
  - Behavior adapts based on what it learned
  - Difficult to understand exactly why decisions are made

The key philosophical difference is about where the intelligence lives. In programming, all the intelligence is in the rules the programmer writes. The computer is just mechanically following instructions. In AI training, the intelligence emerges from the patterns the system discovers in data. The programmer sets up the learning system, but doesn't specify what patterns to find.

Why Training Works: Pattern Discovery

You might wonder: how can showing examples possibly work? How does the system know what patterns to look for? The answer lies in the structure of the learning system and the power of optimization.

The AI system is designed with a flexible structure that can represent many possible patterns. Think of it like a moldable material that can take on different shapes. Initially, it's in a random shape that doesn't correspond to anything useful. But the training process molds it, gradually adjusting its shape based on the examples and feedback.

The mathematical process that does this molding is called optimization. The system's objective is to minimize prediction errors. Every time it makes a wrong guess, that's an error. The optimization process automatically figures out how to adjust the system's internal parameters to reduce these errors. It's like rolling a ball down a hill—the ball naturally moves toward the lowest point. The system naturally evolves toward configurations that make fewer errors.

After seeing thousands of examples, the system has adjusted itself to recognize the patterns that distinguish cats from non-cats. These patterns might include things like:

- Certain shapes that appear in the face region
- Textures that correspond to fur
- Proportions typical of cat bodies
- Colors commonly found in cats
- Relationships between different parts of the image

The system didn't need to be told to look for these things. It discovered them because images with these patterns tended to be labeled "cat" in the training data. The patterns emerged naturally from the data.

The Role of the Human: Curator and Architect

In the training approach, humans still play crucial roles, but they're different from traditional programming:

The Data Curator: Someone needs to gather and label the training examples. For cat recognition, someone needs to collect thousands of images and correctly label which ones contain cats. The quality and quantity of this training data is crucial—if the data is poor, the system will learn poorly. It's like teaching a child; if you show them bad examples or only limited ones, they'll develop a flawed understanding.

The System Architect: Someone needs to design the structure of the AI system itself—what kind of learning system to use, how it should be structured, what kind of patterns it's capable of learning. This requires expertise and is like designing the cognitive architecture that will do the learning.

The Trainer: Someone needs to set up and run the training process—deciding how many examples to use, how many times to go through the data, when to stop training, and so on. This is like being a teacher who designs a curriculum and learning environment.

But notice what the human doesn't do: write the actual rules for recognizing cats. That part emerges from the training process itself. The human provides the environment, structure, and data for learning, but the actual knowledge—the patterns that distinguish cats—is discovered by the system.

Training is More Like Teaching a Person

The training approach to AI is much more similar to how we teach people than how we program computers. When you teach a child to ride a bike, you don't give them explicit rules: "When the bike tilts 3 degrees to the left, shift your weight 2 inches to the right..." That would be absurd and wouldn't work.

Instead, you let them practice. You might give general guidance: "Pedal faster for better balance." You might demonstrate. You might hold the bike steady at first, then gradually let go. But mostly, the child learns through experience. They fall, they adjust, they try again, and gradually they internalize the balance and coordination needed to ride. The learning happens through repetition, feedback, and adjustment.

AI training works the same way. You don't tell the system the rules. You give it practice examples, provide feedback on its performance, and let it adjust through experience. The system gradually internalizes the patterns needed to perform the task.

This is why we call it "training" rather than "programming." You train a dog, you train an athlete, you train a student. Training implies a learning process in which skills develop through practice and feedback rather than through explicit rule-following.

What the System Learns: Implicit Knowledge

After training, what has the AI system learned? This is fascinating and somewhat mysterious. The system has adjusted millions or billions of internal parameters to values that make it good at the task. These parameters collectively encode the patterns it discovered in the training data.

But this knowledge is implicit, not explicit. You can't look at the trained system and read out rules like "cats have pointy ears." The knowledge is distributed across millions of parameters in a way that's not human-readable. The system "knows" how to recognize cats in the sense that it can do so accurately, but it can't explain its knowledge in words or simple rules.

This is actually similar to human knowledge. You know how to ride a bike, but can you explain exactly what muscle movements and balance adjustments you make? You know how to recognize faces, but can you specify the precise features and patterns you use? Much of human knowledge is also implicit—we know how to do things without being able to articulate the rules we're following.

The trained AI system has developed this same kind of implicit knowledge. It has internalized patterns that work, even though those patterns can't be easily extracted or explained.

The Importance of Examples: Garbage In, Garbage Out

In programming, if your rules are correct, your program works correctly. In training, if your examples are good, your system learns well. This makes the training data absolutely critical.

Consider teaching a child about dogs. If you only ever show them pictures of Golden Retrievers, they might think all dogs are large, golden, and fluffy. When they see a Chihuahua, they might not recognize it as a dog. The limitations in their training examples led to limitations in their understanding.

AI has the same issue. If you train a cat recognition system mostly on photos of orange fluffy cats, it might not recognize black cats as well. If all your training photos show cats outdoors in daylight, the system might struggle with indoor photos or nighttime shots. The system can only learn patterns that are present in its training data.

This is why creating good training datasets is so important and often so labor-intensive. You need:

- **Quantity:** Enough examples to cover the diversity of real-world situations
- **Quality:** Correctly labeled examples without errors
- **Diversity:** Examples that represent all the variations you want the system to handle
- **Balance:** Roughly equal numbers of different categories, or the system will be biased toward the more common category

Poor training data leads to poor learning. This is sometimes summarized as "garbage in, garbage out"—if you train on garbage data, you get a garbage system. But with good training data, the system can learn remarkably well.

When Training Beats Programming

Training-based AI excels at problems that have certain characteristics:

Perceptual Tasks: Anything involving recognizing patterns in images, sounds, or other sensory data. Human-written rules for these are nearly impossible, but training works beautifully. Examples: recognizing objects in photos, understanding speech, reading handwritten text.

Complex Pattern Problems: Tasks where patterns exist but are too complex or subtle for humans to specify. Example: predicting which customers will cancel their subscription based on usage patterns.

Problems Where Rules Change: In some domains, the "rules" shift over time or vary by context in ways that are hard to program but can be learned from examples. Example: detecting spam email, where spammers constantly change their tactics.

Human-Like Tasks: Things that humans do easily but struggle to explain how they do them. Example: translating between languages, writing natural-sounding text, playing strategic games.

Tasks With Abundant Data: If you have access to large amounts of example data, training can extract patterns that humans might never notice. Example: analyzing medical images to spot early signs of disease.

When Programming Beats Training

However, training isn't always better. Traditional programming is still preferred when:

Rules Are Clear: If you can specify exactly what should happen in every case, programming is more reliable. Example: calculating taxes based on tax law.

Precision Is Critical: Programmed systems do exactly what you tell them every time. Trained systems might occasionally make mistakes. Example: controlling a spacecraft's navigation.

Data Is Limited: Training requires lots of examples. If you don't have much data, there isn't enough for the system to learn from. Example: designing software for a new, unique situation.

Explainability Is Required: With programming, you can explain exactly why the system made each decision—you just read the code. With training, the reasoning is opaque. Example: legal or medical decisions where you need to justify outcomes.

Consistency Is Essential: Programmed systems will give the same answer to the same input every time. Trained systems might have slight variations. Example: financial calculations that require exact reproducibility.

In practice, many modern systems combine both approaches, using programming for parts where rules are clear and training for parts where pattern learning is needed.

The Training Process: More Details

Let's walk through the training process in more depth to really understand what's happening:

Initial State: Before training, the AI system exists but knows nothing useful. Its millions of parameters are set to random values. It's like a newborn who has the capacity to learn but no knowledge yet.

First Examples: You show the system its first image. Let's say it's a photo of a cat. The system processes the image through its layers of parameters and produces an answer. Because the parameters are random, the answer is essentially a random guess. Maybe it says "12% chance of cat, 88% chance of not cat." You tell it the correct answer was "cat," so it was very wrong.

Learning From Mistakes: The system now performs a crucial operation: it calculates how it should adjust its parameters to do better on this example. There's a mathematical procedure for this (called backpropagation) that figures out which parameters contributed to the error and how to adjust them. The system makes small adjustments to thousands or millions of parameters.

Next Example: You show the system another image, perhaps a dog this time. Again, it makes a prediction, receives feedback, and adjusts its parameters. This process repeats for thousands of examples.

Gradual Improvement: Initially, the adjustments seem random—the system is terrible at the task. But as it sees more examples, patterns start to emerge. Certain parameter settings tend to work better than others. Through the optimization process, these better settings are reinforced. The system gradually improves from random guessing toward meaningful pattern recognition.

Multiple Passes: The system typically goes through the entire dataset many times (these passes are called "epochs"). Each time through, it continues refining its parameters. Eventually, improvements become smaller and smaller as the system approaches the best parameter settings it can achieve with this data.

Convergence: After enough training, the system's performance stabilizes. It has learned what it can from the training data. At this point, you stop training and test the system on new images it has never seen. If training went well, the system will perform well on these new examples too, because it learned general patterns rather than just memorizing the training data.

Overfitting: When Training Goes Wrong

One danger in training is overfitting—when the system learns the training examples too well, essentially memorizing them rather than learning general patterns. It's like a student who memorizes specific test questions and answers but doesn't understand the underlying concepts. They'll ace questions they've seen before but fail on new questions.

Imagine training a cat recognizer on just 100 images. The system might learn to recognize those specific 100 images perfectly—it might even learn subtle details like "image #47 has a blue background and contains a cat." But this doesn't help it recognize cats in new images with different backgrounds.

Good training tries to avoid overfitting by:

- Using lots of diverse training data
- Not training for too long
- Testing on separate data that wasn't used for training
- Using various mathematical techniques to encourage generalization

The goal is for the system to learn general patterns (the essence of cat-ness) rather than specific details of training examples.

Transfer Learning: Building on Prior Training

An interesting technique that bridges training and programming is transfer learning. Once you've trained a system on one task, you can often use that trained system as a starting point for a related task.

For example, suppose you train a system to recognize animals in photos—cats, dogs, birds, horses, etc. That system has learned to recognize features like fur textures, body shapes, and facial features. Now, if you want to build a system to recognize specific dog breeds, you don't need to start from scratch. You can take the animal recognition system and do additional training specifically on dog breeds. The system already knows about animal features in general; it just needs to learn the specific patterns that distinguish breeds.

This is like how humans learn. Once you understand basic math, learning algebra is easier because you build on that foundation. You don't relearn everything from scratch. Transfer learning lets AI systems build on prior training, which can dramatically reduce the amount of new training data needed.

The Human Element in Training

While we say AI systems "learn on their own," there's actually substantial human involvement in the training process:

Data Collection: Humans gather the training data. For image recognition, this means collecting thousands or millions of images. This is often labor-intensive.

Data Labeling: Humans label the training data. For every image, someone needs to identify what's in it. This is tedious work that often involves many people spending many hours on labeling.

System Design: Experts design the architecture of the AI system—deciding what kind of learning approach to use, how to structure it, and what parameters to include. This requires significant expertise and experimentation.

Training Configuration: Humans decide how to train the system—how fast it should learn, how many times to go through the data, when to stop training, and many other choices that affect learning quality.

Evaluation: Humans evaluate whether the trained system works well enough for its intended purpose. They test it, find problems, and decide if more training or different data is needed.

Iteration: Usually, the first trained system isn't good enough. Humans analyze what went wrong, adjust the approach, gather more or better data, and train again. This iteration continues until the system performs acceptably.

So while the actual pattern learning happens automatically, creating a well-trained AI system requires substantial human expertise, judgment, and effort.

Why This Matters: A Paradigm Shift

Understanding that AI is trained rather than programmed helps explain many things about modern AI:

Why it sometimes fails mysteriously: A trained system might fail on examples that seem easy to humans but were poorly represented in the training data. It's not following logical rules; it's applying learned patterns that might not cover every situation.

Why it needs so much data: You can't train without examples, just as you can't learn to play piano without practice. The more data, the better the patterns the system can learn.

Why bias is a concern: If training data reflects human biases—and most real-world data does—the system learns those biases. It's learning patterns from the data, including problematic patterns.

Why it's hard to explain decisions: The system's knowledge is implicit in millions of parameters. There's no simple rule or logic you can point to and say, "This is why it made that decision."

Why it keeps getting better: As we gather more data, develop better training techniques, and design better system architectures, trained AI systems improve. We're not writing better rules; we're enabling better learning.

Why it can do things we can't program: Many tasks that seemed impossible for computers—because we couldn't specify the rules—become possible through training. The system learns patterns we couldn't have articulated.

The Future: Training Becomes the Norm

For decades, programming was the only way to make computers do useful things. But increasingly, training is becoming the preferred approach for many types of problems. Not because programming is bad—it's still excellent for what it does—but because training can solve problems that programming cannot.

As we generate more and more data—from sensors, cameras, text, interactions—we create more opportunities for training AI systems. Every photo uploaded, every video watched, every search performed generates data that could be used to train AI systems to better serve human needs.

As computing power increases, we can train larger systems on more data, learning increasingly sophisticated patterns. Tasks that seem impossibly complex today might become routine for trained AI systems in the future.

Conclusion: A New Way to Make Computers Smart

The shift from programming to training represents a fundamental change in how we create intelligent computer systems. Instead of trying to capture human knowledge as explicit rules and writing them as code, we create systems that can learn patterns from examples, much like humans learn from experience.

This doesn't make programming obsolete—far from it. Programming remains essential for countless applications and is even used to create the learning systems themselves. But training opens new possibilities for tasks that are easy for humans but nearly impossible to program.

When you interact with AI that recognizes your face, understands your voice, recommends products you might like, or generates human-like text, you're benefiting from trained systems. Nobody programmed the rules for how to recognize your specific face or write coherent sentences. The systems learned these capabilities from thousands or millions of examples, discovering patterns that enable them to perform tasks that would be impossibly difficult to program explicitly.

Understanding this distinction—training versus programming—is key to understanding modern AI. It explains both the impressive capabilities of AI systems and their limitations. It helps us appreciate that AI isn't magic or consciousness, but it also isn't just following rules someone programmed. It's something in between: systems that learn patterns from data, developing capabilities through training rather than explicit instruction.

The next time you see AI do something impressive, remember: nobody programmed exactly how to do that. Instead, someone gathered lots of examples, designed a learning system, and trained it to discover the patterns on its own. It's a fundamentally different approach to making computers intelligent, and it's transforming what computers can do, not through better programming, but through better learning.

Four
The Learning Process
How AI Learns Like a Child Through Trial, Error, and Correction

---

Imagine teaching a child to sort shapes. At first, they make mistakes, but you correct them, and they get better. AI does something similar —it makes predictions, gets feedback on what's right or wrong, and adjusts.

When we try to understand how artificial intelligence actually learns, one of the most helpful comparisons is to think about how children learn. Not because AI has consciousness or understanding like a child, but because the fundamental learning mechanism—making attempts, receiving feedback, and adjusting based on that feedback—is remarkably similar. By exploring this parallel in depth, we can truly understand what's happening inside an AI system during the learning process.

How a Child Learns to Sort Shapes

Let's start with a concrete example that most of us can relate to: teaching a young child to sort shapes. Imagine you have a toy with different shaped holes—circles, squares, triangles, and stars—and corresponding blocks in those shapes. Your goal is to teach a two-year-old to put each block through the correct hole.

The First Attempt: You hand the child a circular block. They have no idea what to do. They might try to put it through the square hole—it doesn't fit. They might try the triangle hole—still doesn't fit. Maybe they try the star hole, also wrong. Eventually, by chance or with your guidance, they try the circular hole, and the block goes through. Success!

Providing Feedback: When the child tries the wrong hole, you might say, "No, that doesn't fit. Try another one." When they get it right, you smile and say, "Yes! Good job! The circle goes in the circle hole!" This feedback is crucial—it tells the child which actions worked and which didn't.

The Second Attempt: You give them another circular block. This time, they might remember that the circle went in one particular hole. They might go straight to it, or they might try one or two wrong holes first, but they're already learning. The correct answer is starting to stick in their memory.

Repetition and Patterns: You repeat this process many times. Circles, squares, triangles, stars. At first, every attempt is trial and error. But gradually, something remarkable happens. The child starts to recognize patterns. "These round blocks go in this round hole. These blocks with straight edges go in these holes with straight edges." They don't have words for these patterns yet—they're learning through experience.

Making Mistakes: Even after several successful attempts, the child will still make mistakes. They might grab a square and confidently try to push it through the triangle hole. It doesn't work. You correct them: "Not quite, try a different one." They adjust and try the square hole—success! Each mistake is a learning opportunity.

Getting Better Over Time: After many repetitions over days or weeks, the child becomes proficient. They can quickly and accurately sort all the shapes. They've internalized the patterns. They've learned. And notice: you never sat them down and explained "circles have no corners and constant radius from the center." They learned through experience, feedback, and adjustment.

This entire process—attempting, making mistakes, receiving feedback, adjusting, and gradually improving—is essentially how AI learns.

AI Learning: The Same Process with Different Tools

Now let's see how AI goes through a remarkably similar learning process. We'll use the same example—teaching an AI to classify shapes—to make the parallel clear.

Setting Up the Learning Task: First, we need training data. We create a dataset of thousands of images, each containing a single shape. We label each image: "circle," "square," "triangle," or "star." This dataset is like giving the child many opportunities to practice with the shape-sorting toy.

The First Attempt: We show the AI its first image—let's say it's a circle. The AI has to predict: "What shape is this?"

At this point, the AI knows nothing. Its internal parameters (the numbers that control how it processes information) are set randomly. So its prediction is essentially random. It might output: "30% chance circle, 25% chance square, 25% chance triangle, 20% chance star." It's guessing.

Based on these probabilities, the AI makes its best guess—let's say it predicts "square" because that had a slightly higher probability after its random processing. This is like the child trying to put the circular block through the square hole.

Providing Feedback: We tell the AI the correct answer: "No, that was actually a circle." This is the feedback, just like telling the child, "That doesn't fit, try another."

But here's where AI does something fascinating that children do subconsciously. The AI doesn't just note that it was wrong—it calculates exactly how wrong it was and in what direction. It looks at its prediction (30% circle, 25% square, 25% triangle, 20% star) and compares it to the correct answer (100% circle, 0% square, 0% triangle, 0% star). The difference between these is the error.

Making Adjustments: Now comes the learning step. The AI automatically adjusts its internal parameters to reduce this error. It's figuring out: "What should I change about how I process images so that I would have been more likely to say 'circle' for this particular image?"

The system makes small mathematical adjustments to thousands or millions of internal numbers. These adjustments are calculated to make the AI slightly more likely to correctly identify this circle if it saw it again. It's like the child's brain forming slightly stronger neural connections associated with putting circles in circular holes.

The Second Attempt: We show the AI another image—maybe another circle, or perhaps a square. Again, it makes a prediction, receives feedback on whether it was right or wrong, and adjusts its parameters. This process repeats thousands or millions of times.

Gradual Improvement: At first, the AI is terrible. It's essentially guessing randomly. But after seeing hundreds of examples, something changes. The random adjustments start accumulating in useful directions. The AI begins to recognize patterns: "Images with continuous curved edges tend to be labeled 'circle.' Images with four straight edges at right angles tend to be labeled 'square.'"

These patterns aren't programmed in—the AI is discovering them through the accumulation of many small adjustments based on feedback from many examples.

Still Making Mistakes: Even after significant training, the AI will make mistakes, just like the child. It might see a slightly blurry circle and misclassify it as something else. But each mistake leads to more adjustments, more refinement. The AI is constantly getting feedback and updating its internal model of what distinguishes different shapes.

Achieving Competence: After being trained on thousands of shape images with feedback on each one, the AI becomes quite good at classifying shapes. Show it a new circle it's never seen before, and it will confidently predict "circle." It has learned the patterns that define each shape category.

The Core Learning Loop: Predict, Compare, Adjust

Whether we're talking about a child or an AI, the learning process follows the same basic loop:

1. Make a Prediction/Attempt: Given a situation, try to produce the right answer or action. For a child: try to put the block in a hole. For AI: predict what label applies to the input.

2. Receive Feedback: Get information about whether your attempt was correct. For a child: the block either fits or doesn't, and an adult might comment. For AI: compare the prediction to the correct label provided by trainers.

3. Measure the Error: Determine how wrong you were. For a child: this happens subconsciously—the brain notes the mismatch between expectation and result. For AI: calculate mathematically how different the prediction was from the correct answer.

4. Make Adjustments: Change something about your internal state to do better next time. For a child: neural pathways are strengthened or weakened based on success or failure. For AI: parameters are adjusted mathematically to reduce the error.

5. Repeat: Go back to step 1 with a new example. Both children and AI need many repetitions to learn effectively.

This loop is fundamental to learning, whether biological or artificial. It's called "supervised learning" in AI because each example comes with supervision (feedback) indicating the correct answer.

The Role of Mistakes in Learning

One of the most important insights from comparing AI to child learning is understanding that mistakes are not just acceptable—they're essential for learning.

Why Mistakes Matter for Children: When a child tries to put a square block through a circular hole, and it doesn't fit, that failure provides crucial information. Their brain learns: "This particular action doesn't work in this situation." This negative information is just as valuable as positive information. Without making mistakes, the child wouldn't learn which actions to avoid.

In fact, research on child development shows that children learn most effectively when they're allowed to make mistakes and discover solutions through trial and error, rather than just being told what to do. The active process of attempting, failing, adjusting, and trying again creates stronger learning than passive instruction.

Why Mistakes Matter for AI: The same principle applies to AI. When an AI makes an incorrect prediction, that error drives learning. The system calculates the error and uses it to determine how to adjust its parameters. Without errors, there would be no signal indicating which direction to adjust.

In the early stages of training, an AI makes errors constantly—it's wrong far more often than it's right. But each error provides information that guides the learning process. The system is essentially exploring the space of possible parameter settings, using errors as compass readings that point toward better settings.

The Goldilocks Zone of Mistakes: Interestingly, both children and AI learn best when the task difficulty is in a sweet spot—not too easy, not too hard. If every attempt is wrong, there's too much error, and learning is inefficient. If every attempt is right, there's no error signal to learn from. The ideal learning situation involves being correct sometimes and wrong sometimes, with the balance gradually shifting toward more correct over time.

Feedback: The Teacher's Crucial Role

In our child example, an adult provides feedback—encouragement when correct, gentle correction when wrong. This feedback is what makes learning possible. Without it, the child would just be randomly trying things with no way to know what works.

Feedback for Children: Child development research emphasizes the importance of responsive feedback. When a child succeeds, positive feedback reinforces the behavior. When they fail, corrective feedback (ideally constructive, not harsh) helps them understand what to try instead. The timing matters too—immediate feedback is more effective than delayed feedback because the connection between action and consequence is clearer.

Feedback for AI: In AI training, feedback comes from the labeled training data. Each training example includes both the input (like an image) and the correct output (like the label "circle"). This pairing allows the system to compare its predictions against the correct answers and calculate errors.

The quality of feedback is crucial. If the labels are wrong—if some circles are incorrectly labeled as squares—the AI will learn incorrectly. It's like teaching a child while giving them wrong information. The system learns what it's taught, so accurate feedback is essential.

Different Types of Feedback: Just as children can learn from different types of feedback (verbal praise, physical results like blocks fitting or not, observation of others), AI can learn from different feedback signals:

- **Supervised learning:** Direct labels telling the system the correct answer for each example (like our shape classification task)
- **Reinforcement learning:** Feedback in the form of rewards or penalties based on the consequences of actions (like learning to play a game where you get points for winning)
- **Unsupervised learning:** No explicit labels, but the system learns patterns and structure in the data itself (more like a child learning about the world through exploration)

Adjustment: The Mysterious Inner Change

When a child learns, something changes in their brain. Neural connections are strengthened or weakened, new associations form, and patterns become ingrained. This happens largely unconsciously—the child isn't aware of the neural changes taking place.

How Children Adjust: Neuroscience has shown that learning involves physical changes in the brain. When a child successfully completes a task, neurotransmitters like dopamine reinforce the neural pathways involved. When they fail, different signals may weaken those pathways. Over many repetitions, successful pathways become stronger (more likely to activate) and unsuccessful ones weaken.

The child doesn't consciously decide, "I will now strengthen the neural connection between seeing a round block and reaching for the round hole." It happens automatically through the brain's learning mechanisms. The child just experiences trying, getting feedback, and somehow—mysteriously—getting better over time.

How AI Adjusts: AI systems adjust through mathematical procedures, but the underlying principle remains the same. The system has millions of parameters (numbers) that control how it processes information. These parameters are like the strengths of neural connections in a brain.

When the AI makes a prediction and receives feedback, an algorithm calculates how each parameter should change to reduce the error. The parameters that contributed to the error have been adjusted to improve predictions. Parameters that helped get the right answer are reinforced.

The specific mathematical procedure is called "backpropagation" combined with "gradient descent," but you don't need to understand the math to grasp the concept: the system automatically figures out how to adjust its internal numbers to improve performance, just as a child's brain automatically adjusts its connections.

Small Adjustments Add Up: Both children and AI make small adjustments with each learning experience. A single correction doesn't completely change behavior—a child doesn't perfectly learn to sort shapes after one successful attempt, and an AI doesn't become an expert from one training example. But many small adjustments accumulate into significant learning.

Think of it like wearing away a path through a forest. The first person to walk through makes barely a visible trace. But after hundreds of people walk the same route, a clear path emerges. Each individual's contribution is tiny, but collectively they create something substantial. Learning works similarly—each small adjustment from each training example contributes to the overall learned pattern.

Repetition: The Key to Mastery

Both children and AI require repetition to learn effectively. One-time experiences rarely create lasting learning.

Why Children Need Repetition: Ask any parent or teacher: children need to practice something many times before they master it. This isn't because children are slow—it's because learning is fundamentally a gradual process of adjustment based on accumulated experience.

Each repetition reinforces learning. The first time a child sorts shapes, they're exploring possibilities. The tenth time, they're starting to recognize patterns. The hundredth time, it becomes automatic. Repetition moves learning from conscious effort to unconscious competence.

Psychologists talk about the spacing effect: repeated practice over time leads to better learning than cramming everything into one session. Children learn better with daily practice than with intensive one-time instruction.

Why AI Needs Repetition: AI systems typically process training examples multiple times. The system might go through all 10,000 training images, then go through them all again, and again, and again. Each pass through the data is called an "epoch."

Why multiple passes? Because the adjustments made from each example are small and are influenced by the current state of all parameters. As the parameters evolve, the system can extract different lessons from the same examples. Early in training, the system is learning basic patterns. Later, with better-developed parameters, it can learn more subtle distinctions from the same data.

Just like a child needs to practice sorting shapes many times to master it, an AI needs to process training examples many times to fully learn the patterns they contain.

Generalization: Applying Learning to New Situations

The ultimate test of learning, for both children and AI, is generalization —can you apply what you've learned to new situations you haven't specifically practiced?

Children Generalizing: After a child learns to sort shapes with their shape-sorting toy, they can apply that knowledge to new situations. They might recognize circles in books, squares in windows, triangles on road signs. They haven't practiced with these specific examples, but they've learned general concepts that transfer.

This is true learning—not just memorizing specific cases, but extracting principles that apply broadly. A child who has truly learned what a circle is can recognize circles in countless novel contexts they've never encountered before.

AI Generalizing: The same is true for AI. After training on thousands of shape images, we test the AI on completely new images it has never seen. If training was successful, it will correctly classify these new images. It has learned general patterns (what makes a circle a circle) rather than just memorizing the specific training examples.

Generalization is what makes trained AI systems useful. We don't care if an AI can perfectly recognize the 10,000 images in its training set—we care if it can recognize shapes in the billions of possible images it might encounter in real use. Good generalization means the learned patterns are robust and broadly applicable.

When Generalization Fails: Sometimes children overgeneralize. A child might learn the word "dog" and then call every four-legged animal a dog until they learn finer distinctions. AI can have similar issues—it might learn patterns from training data that don't generalize well to real-world data if the training examples weren't diverse enough.

This is why diverse training data is important. If you only show a child one type of dog, they'll have a limited understanding. If you only train an AI on one type of image, it will struggle with other types. Good generalization requires experience with variety.

The Timeline of Learning: From Confusion to Competence

Let's trace the typical trajectory of learning for both children and AI:

Phase 1: Complete Confusion (Days 1-5 for children, Early epochs for AI): The learner has no idea what they're doing. Attempts are essentially random. The child tries every hole for every block with no pattern. The AI's predictions are barely better than chance. Errors are frequent and large. This phase can be frustrating for children (and their parents), but it is a necessary starting point.

Phase 2: Glimmers of Understanding (Days 5-15 for children, Middle epochs for AI): Occasionally, the learner gets it right, and these successes start to form patterns. The child sometimes goes straight to the correct hole, though they're inconsistent. The AI's predictions show some correlation with the correct answers—it's slightly better than random guessing. Both are starting to extract patterns from their experiences.

Phase 3: Developing Competence (Weeks 2-4 for children, Later epochs for AI): The learner is right more often than wrong. The child correctly sorts shapes most of the time, with occasional mistakes. The AI's accuracy might be 70-80%, which is significantly better than the 25%

it would get by random guessing. Both are clearly learning, though not yet masters.

Phase 4: Reliable Performance (Week 4+ for children, End of training for AI): The learner has achieved a high level of competence. The child quickly and confidently sorts all shapes correctly nearly every time. The AI achieves 95%+ accuracy on new examples. Both have internalized the patterns well enough for consistent performance.

Phase 5: Automatic Expertise (Months later for children, After deployment for AI): With enough practice, the skill becomes effortless and automatic. The child doesn't consciously think about sorting shapes —they just do it. The AI processes new images almost instantly with high confidence. The learned skill has become ingrained.

What Makes Learning Effective: Lessons from Both Children and AI

Researchers studying both child development and AI have discovered remarkably similar principles for effective learning:

Quality of Examples Matters: Children learn better from clear, varied examples than from ambiguous or repetitive ones. If a child only ever sees one red circle, they might think all circles are red. AI has the same issue—the diversity and quality of training examples directly impact what's learned.

Feedback Needs to Be Clear: Children benefit from clear, consistent feedback. Ambiguous or contradictory feedback confuses them. AI also requires clear, correct labels. If training data has errors or inconsistencies, the AI learns poorly.

The Right Pace: Children can be overwhelmed if learning moves too fast, or bored if it goes too slow. Finding the right pace for the individual learner is important. AI has similar considerations—learning rates that are too fast can cause unstable learning, while rates too slow make training inefficiently long.

Engagement and Attention: Children learn better when they're engaged and paying attention. While AI doesn't have attention or motivation in the human sense, there are analogous concepts—the system needs to focus its learning capacity on the relevant features of the input, rather than being distracted by irrelevant noise.

Building on Prior Knowledge: Children learn new things more easily when they connect to what they already know. AI can use "transfer learning"—starting with a system already trained on related tasks, then adapting it to a new task. Both benefit from building on foundations rather than starting from scratch.

Mistakes Are Opportunities: Both children and AI learn more from mistakes than from easy successes. When everything is too easy, there's nothing to learn. The challenges and errors drive improvement.

The Emotional Dimension: Where Children and AI Diverge

Up to this point, we've focused on the remarkable similarities between child learning and AI learning. But there's a crucial difference worth acknowledging: the emotional and experiential aspect of learning.

Children's Learning Experience: When a child learns to sort shapes, they experience frustration when they fail, joy when they succeed, pride in mastery, and pleasure in the activity (especially when it's playful). These emotions are part of what motivates continued learning. Children also understand, at some level, what they're doing. They know they're putting shapes in holes, even if they can't articulate the patterns they're learning.

Learning for children is embedded in a rich context of physical sensation, social interaction, emotional response, and emerging understanding. It's a holistic experience involving their whole developing person.

AI's "Experience": AI has none of this. When an AI adjusts its parameters in response to feedback, there's no frustration, no joy, no feeling at all. There's no understanding or awareness of what it's doing. The AI doesn't "know" it's learning to classify shapes, doesn't "want" to get better, doesn't "feel" anything about its progress.

The adjustments are made through pure mathematical calculation. The system is optimizing numbers to minimize error functions. There's no subjective experience accompanying this process. It's learning without a learner, in the conscious sense.

This is important to remember: when we say AI learns "like a child," we mean the functional process—predict, feedback, adjust, repeat—is similar. But the experiential reality is utterly different. AI is learning without awareness, understanding, or emotion.

Practical Implications of Understanding AI Learning

Understanding that AI learns through prediction, feedback, and adjustment has important practical implications:

Training Data is Critical: Just as the experiences you provide to a child shape what they learn, the training data you provide to an AI determines what it learns. Biased data produces biased AI. Limited data produces limited capabilities. High-quality, diverse data produces more capable, fair systems.

AI Learns What You Teach: Children learn what they're exposed to, for better or worse. If a child is exposed to negative stereotypes, they may internalize them. AI is similar—it learns the patterns in its training data, including problematic patterns. If training data reflects human biases, the AI will learn those biases.

Learning Takes Time and Resources: Just as you can't expect a child to master something in one sitting, you can't train an AI with minimal data or computation. Effective learning requires sufficient examples, repetition, and processing. Training large AI systems can take days or weeks on powerful computers.

Testing is Essential: You wouldn't assume a child has mastered a skill without testing them on new examples. Similarly, AI must be tested on data it hasn't seen during training to verify that it has genuinely learned generalizable patterns rather than just memorizing training examples.

Continuous Learning: Children continue learning throughout life. Some AI systems can also continue learning after initial training, adjusting based on new examples and feedback. This allows them to improve and adapt over time, though it must be managed carefully to prevent "catastrophic forgetting," in which learning new things erases prior learning.

Different Learning Tasks, Same Basic Process

The shape-sorting example is simple, but the same learning process applies to far more complex tasks:

Image Recognition: Training AI to recognize objects in photos works the same way. Show the system millions of labeled images, let it make predictions, provide feedback, allow adjustments. It learns to recognize cats, cars, people, and countless other objects through this process.

Language Understanding: Large language AI models learn to predict the next word in a sentence by being trained on billions of examples of text. They make predictions, compare them to the actual next word, and adjust. Through this process, they learn grammar, facts, reasoning patterns, and how to generate coherent text.

Game Playing: AI systems that play games like chess or Go learn by playing millions of games. They make moves (predictions), see the outcomes (feedback), and adjust their strategy. Through countless iterations, they learn to play at superhuman levels.

Speech Recognition: AI learns to transcribe speech by training on hours of recorded audio paired with transcripts. It predicts what words were spoken, compares them to the correct transcript, and adjusts. It learns to recognize words despite accents, background noise, and speech variation.

In every case, the core loop is the same: predict, get feedback, adjust, repeat. The specific details vary, but the fundamental learning mechanism is consistent.

The Wonder of Emergent Ability

One of the most remarkable aspects of learning—both for children and AI—is that complex abilities can emerge from simple, repeated processes.

Children's Emergent Abilities: A child learning to sort shapes is exercising cognitive abilities that will later support math, spatial reasoning, categorization, and abstract thinking. They're not just learning about shapes—they're developing general learning capabilities. Parents often marvel at how children suddenly seem to "get" concepts after accumulated practice, as if understanding crystallizes all at once from gradual preparation.

AI's Emergent Abilities: Similarly, AI systems sometimes develop abilities that weren't explicitly trained. A language model trained only to predict next words can somehow also translate languages, answer questions, write poetry, and reason through problems—capabilities that emerge from the general patterns learned through next-word prediction.

These emergent abilities arise because the learning process doesn't just memorize specific answers—it builds internal representations and patterns that turn out to be useful for many related tasks. Both children and AI develop more than they're explicitly taught.

Conclusion: Learning as a Universal Process

The comparison between how children learn and how AI learns reveals something profound: learning, at its core, might be a universal process that transcends the specific substrate (biological brains or silicon computers).

Whether we're talking about a toddler learning to sort shapes or an AI system learning to classify images, the fundamental process is the same:

1. **Make an attempt** at the task based on current knowledge
2. **Receive feedback** about whether the attempt was correct
3. **Measure the error** or gap between the attempt and the correct answer
4. **Adjust internal parameters** to reduce that error
5. **Repeat many times** until competence develops

This process works. It's how children learn practically everything during their development—language, motor skills, social behaviors, and academic subjects. And it's how AI systems learn to perform tasks that would be nearly impossible to program explicitly.

The key insight is that intelligence—at least certain types of intelligent behavior—can emerge from the accumulation of many small adjustments driven by feedback on many practice attempts. You don't need to understand the task fully from the beginning. You don't need perfect performance immediately. You just need a system capable of adjustment, a source of feedback, and enough repetition.

For children, this learning process is supported by biological systems that evolved over millions of years, embedded in rich emotional and social contexts, and leading to genuine understanding and consciousness. For AI, the learning process is implemented through mathematical optimization, occurring without any subjective experience, and producing capable behavior without genuine understanding.

But in both cases, the practical mechanism is surprisingly similar: predict, get feedback, adjust, repeat. From these simple steps, iterated thousands or millions of times, genuine capability emerges. The child becomes competent at sorting shapes and eventually develops sophisticated intelligence. The AI becomes accurate at its trained task and can sometimes display surprisingly sophisticated behavior.

Understanding this parallel helps us appreciate both the power of AI—it can learn things we can't easily program—and its limitations—it learns what it's trained on, can make mistakes, and lacks the understanding and flexibility of human intelligence. The AI is learning, genuinely learning, through a process functionally similar to how we learned as children. But it's learning without the consciousness, emotion, motivation, and understanding that made our childhood learning such a rich human experience.

When you interact with an AI system, remember: it got good at what it does through a process of making millions of predictions, receiving feedback on each one, and adjusting itself bit by bit based on that feedback. Just like you learned, through many attempts and corrections, to do the countless things you now do effortlessly. The process is universal, even if the learners are profoundly different.

Five
AI Is Already Everywhere in Your Life
The Invisible Intelligence Surrounding You

Your phone's facial recognition, Netflix recommendations, spam filters, voice assistants, GPS navigation, even the autocorrect fixing your typos—that's all AI working behind the scenes.

Most people think of artificial intelligence as something futuristic, something that exists primarily in science fiction movies or research laboratories. The reality is startlingly different: AI is already woven throughout your daily life in ways you probably don't even notice. Every day, you interact with dozens of AI systems, relying on them for convenience, safety, entertainment, and efficiency. Let's explore the invisible intelligence that surrounds you from the moment you wake up until you go to sleep.

Morning: Your Day Begins with AI

Your Alarm and Sleep Tracking

Your day likely begins with AI before you're even conscious. If you use a smartphone with a smart alarm feature, AI has been monitoring your sleep cycles throughout the night. These systems use motion sensors and, sometimes, sound to detect whether you're in light sleep or deep sleep. The AI learns your sleep patterns over time and tries to wake you during a light sleep phase within a window around your target wake time, making waking up feel more natural and less jarring.

Some fitness trackers and smartwatches go further, using AI to analyze your heart rate, movement patterns, and even breathing to provide detailed sleep quality reports. The AI has learned what healthy sleep patterns look like from data from millions of users and compares your patterns to identify potential issues.

Unlocking Your Phone

When you pick up your phone and look at the screen, AI instantly recognizes your face and unlocks the device. This facial recognition technology is a sophisticated AI system that has learned what your face looks like from multiple angles, in different lighting conditions, and even as your appearance changes over time (new haircut, glasses, facial hair, aging).

The system takes an image from the front camera, identifies key facial features and their spatial relationships, and compares this to the stored mathematical representation of your face. It does this in a fraction of a second, accurately enough to distinguish you from billions of other people, even from your identical twin in many cases. The AI has learned to focus on the features that remain constant despite changes in expression, lighting, or minor appearance changes.

Checking Your Notifications

As you scroll through your notifications, AI has already been at work deciding which ones to show you prominently. Your phone's operating system uses AI to learn which apps and contacts are most important to you based on your interaction patterns. It prioritizes notifications accordingly and may even suppress notifications it predicts you won't care about at this moment.

If you use email, an AI spam filter has already screened your inbox, identifying and removing junk mail before you even see it. This filter has learned to recognize patterns in spam emails—suspicious sender addresses, certain phrases commonly used in scams, formatting typical of phishing attempts—and blocks them automatically. It's constantly learning too, adjusting as spammers change their tactics.

Getting Ready: AI Assists Your Morning Routine

Voice Assistants

Many people use voice assistants like Siri, Alexa, or Google Assistant in the morning. When you say, "Hey Siri, what's the weather today?" several AI systems spring into action:

First, speech recognition AI converts your spoken words into text. This system has learned to understand human speech despite accents, background noise, and natural variations in how people speak. It breaks down the audio into phonemes, identifies words, and constructs the sentence you spoke.

Then, natural language understanding AI interprets what you meant. It determines that you're asking a question about weather and that "today" refers to the current date and your current location (which it knows from GPS).

Finally, another AI system formulates a natural-sounding response and converts it back to speech using text-to-speech AI that has learned to sound human-like rather than robotic.

All of this happens in seconds, involving multiple AI systems working together seamlessly.

Smart Home Devices

If you have smart home devices, AI is controlling your environment. Smart thermostats use AI to learn your schedule and temperature preferences, automatically adjusting heating and cooling to be comfortable when you're home and save energy when you're away. The system learns patterns like "they usually wake up at 7 am on weekdays and like the house at 72 degrees by then."

Smart lights might gradually brighten in the morning, with AI having learned your typical wake-up time. Smart coffee makers might start brewing when AI detects that you've gotten out of bed, based on motion sensors or your phone's location.

Commute: AI Gets You Where You're Going

GPS Navigation

When you open Google Maps, Apple Maps, or Waze to navigate somewhere, you're relying on incredibly sophisticated AI. These systems do far more than just show you the shortest route—they predict traffic conditions, suggest optimal routes, and constantly adjust based on real-time conditions.

The AI analyzes current traffic data from millions of users, historical traffic patterns (traffic is usually heavy on this road at this time on Tuesdays), weather conditions, accidents, road closures, and construction. It predicts how long each possible route will take and recommends the best one. As you drive, if traffic changes, the AI recalculates and may suggest a different route.

These navigation systems have learned complex patterns: where traffic bottlenecks typically occur, how long delays usually last, which alternate routes are effective, and even how driving patterns differ by time of day, day of week, and season.

Ride-Sharing Apps

If you use Uber or Lyft, AI matches you with drivers, calculates prices based on demand, predicts arrival times, and optimizes routes. The pricing AI has learned to predict demand patterns and adjust prices accordingly (surge pricing). The matching AI decides which driver should pick you up based on proximity, destination, driver ratings, and other factors.

Music Streaming

During your commute, you might stream music on Spotify, Apple Music, or YouTube Music. The songs that appear in your personalized playlists and recommendations are chosen by an AI that has learned your musical preferences. These systems analyze what songs you listen to, which you skip, which you replay, and what time of day you listen to different genres.

The AI also looks at what similar users enjoy (collaborative filtering) and analyzes the musical characteristics of songs themselves (tempo, key, instrumentation, vocal style) to find music that matches your taste. The "Discover Weekly" playlist on Spotify, for example, is entirely generated by AI that has learned to predict what songs you'll enjoy but haven't heard yet.

Podcast Recommendations

Similarly, if you listen to podcasts, AI is recommending episodes based on your listening history, what you finish versus abandon, and what similar listeners enjoy. Some podcast apps even use AI to generate custom playlists of podcast episodes on topics you care about.

At Work or School: AI Enhances Productivity

Email Management

Once you're at work or school, AI continues to assist throughout your day. Your email client uses multiple AI systems:

- **Spam filtering** blocks unwanted mail.

- **Priority inbox** features use AI to identify which emails are most important based on who sent them, the content, and your typical response patterns.
- **Smart replies** suggest quick responses, with AI generating contextually appropriate short replies like "Thanks, I'll look into it" or "Sounds good, see you then."
- **Calendar integration** AI can detect when an email mentions a meeting and suggest adding it to your calendar.
- **Phishing detection** AI identifies suspicious emails that might be trying to steal your information.

Autocorrect and Predictive Text

Every time you type on your phone or computer, AI is helping you. Autocorrect uses AI that has learned common typing errors, correct spellings, and contextually appropriate words. When you type "teh," it knows you meant "the." When you type "your" in a context that requires "you're," more advanced systems can catch that.

Predictive text suggestions appearing above your keyboard are AI predictions of what word you'll type next, based on what you've typed so far, your personal writing patterns, and common phrase patterns in language. The AI has learned from massive amounts of text data how people typically construct sentences.

Grammar Checkers

Tools like Grammarly use sophisticated AI not just to check spelling but to analyze grammar, style, tone, and clarity. The AI has learned the rules of English grammar, common writing mistakes, and stylistic conventions. It can suggest that "very unique" should be just "unique" (since unique is absolute), that your sentence is too long and complex, or that your tone seems aggressive when you intended to be professional.

Document Search

When you search for a file on your computer or in cloud storage, AI helps you find it even if you don't remember the exact name. The AI indexes the content of your documents, learns which files you access frequently, and predicts what you're looking for based on partial queries. It might suggest "Q3 Sales Report 2024" when you just type "sales."

Video Conferencing

If you use Zoom, Teams, or other video conferencing tools, AI is working in the background:

- **Background blur or replacement** uses AI to distinguish you from your background in real-time, even as you move
- **Noise cancellation** AI filters out background sounds like barking dogs, sirens, or keyboard typing while preserving your voice
- **Auto-framing** AI keeps you centered in the frame even if you move around
- **Live captions** use speech recognition AI to transcribe what people are saying in real-time

Midday: AI in Your Social Media and Entertainment

Social Media Feeds

When you check Facebook, Instagram, Twitter, TikTok, or any social media platform, AI is curating what you see. The days of seeing every post from everyone you follow in chronological order are gone—AI now decides what appears in your feed and in what order.

These AI systems learn what kinds of content you engage with. Do you often watch cooking videos? You'll see more of those. Do you frequently comment on posts from certain friends? You'll see more of their content. Do you quickly scroll past political posts? You'll see fewer of them.

The AI is optimizing for "engagement"—keeping you on the platform as long as possible. It has learned, from data on millions of users, what types of content keep people scrolling, and what makes them like, comment, and share. This has profound effects on what information people see and how they understand the world.

Content Moderation

Behind the scenes, AI is also moderating content on these platforms. Billions of pieces of content are posted daily—far too much for human moderators to review. AI systems scan posts, images, and videos to detect prohibited content: hate speech, graphic violence, spam, nudity, misinformation, and more.

These AI systems have been trained on examples of policy-violating content to recognize patterns. They automatically remove some content and flag other content for human review. While imperfect—sometimes catching innocent content or missing violations—these systems handle the vast majority of moderation at a scale that would be impossible for humans alone.

Photo Organization and Editing

The Photos app on your phone uses AI extensively. It automatically organizes your photos by:

- **Face recognition:** Identifying which photos contain which people
- **Object recognition:** Finding all photos containing dogs, beaches, food, etc.
- **Scene detection:** Categorizing photos as sunsets, landscapes, documents, screenshots, etc.

- **Quality assessment:** Identifying your best photos to feature in memories or highlights

When you edit photos, many enhancement features use AI. The "enhance" button uses AI that has learned what makes photos look good, and automatically adjusts brightness, contrast, saturation, and other parameters. Portrait mode blur uses AI to detect depth and separate the subject from the background. Some apps can remove unwanted objects from photos, intelligently filling in the background with AI.

Video Streaming Recommendations

Netflix, YouTube, Hulu, Disney+, and other streaming services rely heavily on AI to recommend content. Netflix's recommendation AI is famous—it analyzes what you watch, how long you watch it, what time of day you watch different genres, what you rate highly, what you start but don't finish, and patterns from millions of other users.

The AI has learned complex patterns: people who loved this show often love these other shows; people who watch comedies on weekday evenings often watch dramas on weekend nights; if someone starts a series and watches three episodes in a row, they'll probably finish it. About 80% of what people watch on Netflix comes from recommendations, making this AI crucial to the business.

YouTube's AI is perhaps even more influential, suggesting what video to watch next. This AI has learned to predict what will keep you watching, which has been both praised (helping people discover content they love) and criticized (potentially creating filter bubbles or recommending increasingly extreme content).

Afternoon: AI in Shopping and Finance

Online Shopping

When you shop online on Amazon, eBay, or other sites, AI is everywhere:

- **Product recommendations:** "Customers who bought this also bought..." is AI predicting what you might want based on patterns from millions of other shoppers
- **Personalized homepages:** The products shown on your homepage are AI-selected based on your browsing and purchase history
- **Price optimization:** Some retailers use AI to dynamically adjust prices based on demand, competition, and your likelihood to purchase
- **Search results:** When you search for "comfortable shoes," AI ranks results based on what "comfortable" likely means to you specifically
- **Chatbots:** Customer service chatbots use AI to understand your question and provide relevant answers
- **Fraud detection:** AI monitors transactions for suspicious patterns that might indicate credit card fraud

Advertising

The ads you see online are almost always AI-selected. Advertising platforms use AI to:

- Predict which ads you're most likely to click on or respond to
- Choose optimal times to show you ads when you're most receptive
- Customize ad creative for different audiences
- Measure ad effectiveness and automatically adjust campaigns

This is why you might search for "hiking boots" and then see hiking boot ads for days afterward—the AI has identified you as someone currently interested in that product.

Banking and Finance Apps

If you use banking apps, AI is working to protect you and help you manage money:

- **Fraud detection:** AI monitors your transactions for unusual patterns—purchases in unusual locations, spending amounts out of character, transaction patterns typical of stolen cards
- **Spending insights:** Apps that categorize your spending and provide insights use AI to identify what each transaction was for
- **Credit score factors:** Credit scoring systems increasingly use AI to assess creditworthiness
- **Investment apps:** Robo-advisors use AI to create and manage investment portfolios based on your risk tolerance and goals
- **Bill predictions:** Apps that predict upcoming bills and cash flow use AI that has learned your financial patterns

Evening: AI in Your Home and Leisure

Smart Home Evening Routines

As evening approaches, your smart home AI might automatically adjust lighting to warmer tones, lower the thermostat slightly, and begin other routines it has learned you prefer in the evening. Some systems can detect when you arrive home and automatically unlock doors, turn on lights, and adjust climate control.

Security cameras with AI can distinguish between a person, a car, an animal, and a package, alerting you only to the types of movement you care about. They can even recognize familiar faces versus strangers.

Cooking Assistance

If you search for recipes online, AI is recommending recipes based on your past searches, dietary preferences, and what similar users enjoyed. Some apps can identify food from photos and suggest recipes. Smart ovens use AI to recognize what you're cooking and adjust temperature and timing automatically.

Gaming

Video games use AI extensively. The non-player characters (NPCs) you interact with use AI to behave somewhat intelligently—enemies that hunt you, allies that assist you, and characters that respond to your choices. The difficulty adjustment in many games uses AI to keep gameplay challenging but not frustrating, learning your skill level and adjusting accordingly.

Fitness and Health Tracking

Fitness trackers and health apps use AI constantly:

- **Activity recognition:** Automatically detecting whether you're walking, running, cycling, or swimming
- **Heart rate analysis:** Identifying patterns that might indicate health issues
- **Sleep quality assessment:** Analyzing movement and heart rate to determine sleep stages
- **Workout recommendations:** Suggesting exercises based on your goals, past workouts, and progress
- **Calorie estimation:** Estimating calories burned based on activity type, intensity, and your physical characteristics

Some apps can even analyze photos of your meals to estimate calorie content and nutritional information.

Night: AI Helps You Wind Down

Evening Entertainment

Your evening entertainment continues to be AI-curated. Streaming music for relaxation, podcast recommendations for bedtime, even the queue of videos or shows lined up for you—all selected by AI that has learned your evening preferences.

Reading Apps

E-reader apps like Kindle use AI to recommend books based on what you've read and enjoyed. The "customers who bought this also bought" recommendations are AI identifying patterns in millions of readers' preferences.

Some apps use AI to adjust text size, spacing, and background color for optimal readability based on ambient lighting and your vision needs.

Sleep Assistance

Apps that play white noise, nature sounds, or sleep stories often use AI to learn which sounds help you fall asleep fastest and sleep most soundly. Some can adjust volume throughout the night as your sleep stages change.

Sleep-tracking AI monitors your sleep patterns and can identify issues like potential sleep apnea, providing insights that might prompt you to seek medical attention.

The AI You Don't See: Infrastructure and Services

Beyond the consumer-facing AI you directly interact with, countless AI systems work in the background to keep modern society functioning:

Electrical Grid Management

AI systems help manage the power grid, predicting demand, optimizing power generation and distribution, and detecting faults before they cause outages. These systems have learned patterns in electricity usage and can predict surges before they happen.

Traffic Light Optimization

Many cities use AI to control traffic lights, adjusting timing based on real-time traffic flow to minimize congestion. The AI has learned traffic patterns and can adapt to unusual situations like accidents or events.

Weather Forecasting

Modern weather prediction relies heavily on AI analyzing massive amounts of data from satellites, weather stations, and sensors to predict future conditions. AI has learned complex atmospheric patterns and can identify signs of approaching storms, temperature changes, and other weather events.

Spam and Cyber Security

Beyond your personal spam filter, AI systems protect internet infrastructure from spam, malware, and cyberattacks. These systems analyze billions of emails, web requests, and network packets to identify threats, learning to recognize new attack patterns as they emerge.

Language Translation

Services like Google Translate use sophisticated AI that has learned to translate between languages by studying millions of translated documents. The AI learns not just word-for-word translation but how to preserve meaning, handle idioms, and adjust for cultural context.

Emergency Services

Some 911 systems use AI to help prioritize calls, dispatch appropriate resources, and even provide guidance to callers before help arrives. The AI has learned from historical data about different types of emergencies and optimal responses.

Healthcare: AI Saving Lives

Diagnostic Assistance

Hospitals and clinics increasingly use AI to assist in diagnosis. AI systems can:

- Analyze medical images (X-rays, MRIs, CT scans) to detect tumors, fractures, or anomalies, often spotting things human doctors might miss
- Predict patient deterioration by monitoring vital signs and identifying patterns that precede serious events
- Recommend treatments based on patient characteristics, symptoms, and outcomes from similar patients
- Identify drug interactions and potential side effects

Drug Discovery

AI is accelerating the discovery of new medications by predicting which molecules might be effective against specific diseases, dramatically reducing the time and cost of early-stage drug development.

Personal Health Monitoring

Smartwatches with AI can detect irregular heart rhythms that might indicate atrial fibrillation, potentially preventing strokes. Some can detect falls and automatically call for help. The AI has learned what abnormal patterns look like in physiological data.

The Scope of AI in Your Life: A Typical Day

Let's count the AI systems an average person might interact with in a single day:

Morning (6am-9am): Sleep tracking, alarm optimization, facial recognition unlock, notification prioritization, spam filtering, voice assistant, smart home automation, weather forecasting, GPS navigation, ride-sharing, music recommendations—roughly 11 AI systems.

Work/School (9am-5pm): Email management, autocorrect, predictive text, grammar checking, document search, video conferencing AI, calendar optimization, fraud detection in any purchases—roughly 8 more AI systems.

Evening (5pm-10pm): Social media feeds (multiple platforms), content moderation, photo organization, streaming recommendations (music, video, podcasts), online shopping, ad targeting, smart home automation, security cameras, cooking assistance, gaming AI, fitness tracking—roughly 15 AI systems.

Night (10pm-6am): Sleep assistance, sleep tracking, smart home automation—roughly 3 AI systems.

That's potentially 37 different AI systems in a typical day, and this is likely an underestimate. Many people interact with dozens more depending on their specific apps, services, and devices.

Why Is AI So Prevalent?

AI has become ubiquitous for several reasons:

- **It Solves Real Problems:** Each AI system addresses a genuine need—reducing spam, helping navigation, protecting against fraud, and finding content you'll enjoy. These are valuable services that improve people's lives.

- **It Scales Efficiently:** Once an AI system is trained, it can serve millions or billions of users with relatively low marginal cost. This makes it economically attractive for companies to develop AI solutions.
- **Data Abundance:** The digital age generates enormous amounts of data, which AI can learn from. Every interaction online, every photo taken, every search query generates data that can train AI systems.
- **Computing Power:** Modern computers and especially GPUs are powerful enough to run sophisticated AI in real-time, making AI-powered features responsive enough for practical use.
- **Competitive Advantage:** Companies that effectively use AI can provide better services, attract more users, and operate more efficiently than competitors who don't. This creates strong incentives to implement AI.
- **User Expectations:** People now expect smart features—accurate voice recognition, good recommendations, automatic photo organization. Not having these AI-powered features makes a product feel outdated.

The Invisible Nature of AI

Most AI in your life is invisible by design. You don't think "I'm now using artificial intelligence" when you unlock your phone with your face or get directions from Google Maps. The AI fades into the background, becoming just part of how these tools work.

This invisibility is intentional. Good design makes technology feel natural and effortless. The complex AI doing face recognition, traffic prediction, or recommendation generation is hidden behind simple, intuitive interfaces.

This invisibility has pros and cons. On the positive side, it makes technology accessible to everyone regardless of technical knowledge. You don't need to understand machine learning to benefit from it. On the negative side, it can make people unaware of how much AI is shaping their experiences, what data is being collected, and what limitations or biases these systems might have.

The Impact on Daily Life

The prevalence of AI in daily life has profound effects:

- **Convenience:** AI makes countless tasks faster, easier, and more convenient. Finding information, getting places, communicating, shopping, and entertainment are all enhanced by AI.
- **Personalization:** AI enables experiences tailored to individual preferences in ways that would be impossible manually. Your music, your news, your recommendations—all customized for you.
- **Efficiency:** AI helps us accomplish more in less time by automating routine tasks, filtering information, and optimizing processes.
- **Access:** AI makes capabilities available to everyone that previously required expertise. Everyone has a personal assistant (voice AI), everyone has access to language translation, and everyone can edit photos professionally.
- **Dependence:** We've become quite dependent on these AI systems. Try navigating a new city without GPS, finding information without search engines, or communicating without autocorrect—it's now surprisingly difficult.
- **Privacy Considerations:** AI that personalizes your experience requires data about you. Many people don't realize how much data is collected or how it's used to train and operate AI systems.
- **Filter Bubbles:** AI that shows you what you're likely to engage

with can create echo chambers where you primarily see information that confirms your existing views.

Looking Forward: Even More AI

The AI in your life today is just the beginning. Upcoming developments will bring AI even deeper into daily life:

- **AI assistants** will become more capable, handling complex tasks like planning vacations, managing schedules, and making purchases
- **Autonomous vehicles** will use AI to navigate, potentially changing transportation fundamentally
- **Healthcare AI** will provide increasingly sophisticated monitoring and diagnostic support
- **Education AI** will offer personalized tutoring and adapt to individual learning styles
- **Creative AI** will assist in writing, art, music, and design
- **Work AI** will handle more routine tasks, changing what kinds of work humans do

Conclusion: AI as Everyday Technology

Artificial intelligence isn't something futuristic or rare—it's already deeply embedded in your daily life. From the moment your smart alarm wakes you until your sleep tracker monitors your rest, AI systems are working constantly, mostly invisibly, to make your life more convenient, efficient, and personalized.

Your phone, computer, car, home, entertainment, communication, shopping, navigation, work, and leisure all involve multiple AI systems. You interact with dozens of AI applications daily, usually without thinking of them as AI. They've become simply how things work.

Understanding this prevalence of AI is important for several reasons. It helps you appreciate the technology you use, make informed decisions about privacy and data sharing, recognize the limitations and potential biases of AI systems, and participate meaningfully in conversations about how AI should be developed and regulated.

The AI surrounding you today was science fiction just a few decades ago. It demonstrates how quickly technology can move from laboratories to ubiquitous daily use. As AI continues to advance, even more of your life will be touched by these intelligent systems.

Whether this excites or concerns you likely depends on your perspective, but one thing is certain: AI is not coming someday—it's already here, already everywhere, already shaping your daily experience in countless visible and invisible ways. The future of AI isn't something to wait for; it's something we're living in right now, every day, with every interaction with our increasingly intelligent devices and services.

Six

There Are Different Types of AI

Understanding the Spectrum from Narrow to General Intelligence

---

Some AI is "narrow"—really good at one specific thing, like playing chess or recognizing speech. Then there's the idea of "general" AI that could handle any task like humans do, but that doesn't exist yet.

When most people hear about artificial intelligence, they often imagine a single type of technology—perhaps a humanoid robot or a superintelligent computer that can do anything. But the reality of AI is much more nuanced. There are fundamentally different types of AI, each with very different capabilities, limitations, and implications. Understanding these distinctions is crucial for grasping what AI can and cannot do, both today and in the foreseeable future.

The Fundamental Distinction: Narrow vs. General AI

The most important distinction in AI is between narrow AI (also called weak AI or specialized AI) and general AI (also called strong AI or artificial general intelligence, AGI). This distinction isn't just technical—it's the difference between a tool that does one thing well and an intelligence that can think flexibly across any domain, like humans do.

Narrow AI refers to AI systems designed and trained to perform specific tasks. These systems can be extraordinarily good at their designated task—sometimes far better than humans—but they cannot transfer their capabilities to other domains. They're specialists, not generalists.

General AI refers to a theoretical AI that would have human-like ability to understand, learn, and apply intelligence across any domain. This AI could learn new skills, adapt to novel situations, reason abstractly, and transfer knowledge from one area to another—all things humans do naturally, but current AI cannot.

The critical fact: All AI that exists today is narrow AI. General AI remains theoretical, a goal researchers are working toward but haven't achieved. This distinction cannot be overstated, because much of the confusion about AI comes from conflating what narrow AI can do with what people imagine general AI might do.

Narrow AI: The Specialists All Around Us

Let's deeply explore narrow AI, since it's what actually exists and what you interact with daily.

What Makes AI "Narrow"

Narrow AI is called narrow because its intelligence is confined to a narrow domain. It's like having a savant who is a genius at one thing but has no ability outside that specialty. The system has been specifically designed and trained for a particular task, and that's all it can do.

Consider a chess-playing AI like Deep Blue (the IBM system that defeated world champion Garry Kasparov in 1997) or more recent chess engines like Stockfish or AlphaZero. These systems play chess at superhuman levels. They can evaluate millions of positions per second, plan dozens of moves ahead, and defeat any human player with ease.

But here's what's crucial: that same chess AI cannot play checkers. It cannot play Go. It cannot recognize images. It cannot understand language. It cannot do anything except play chess. If you tried to use it for any other purpose, it would be completely useless. Its intelligence is entirely narrow—focused on chess and only chess.

This might seem obvious once stated, but it reveals something profound about narrow AI: it doesn't "understand" chess in the way humans do. It has no concept of strategy in any general sense, no ability to transfer its planning abilities to other domains. It's extraordinarily good at the specific pattern recognition and evaluation required for chess, but that's the extent of its capability.

Examples of Narrow AI in Different Domains

To really understand narrow AI, let's look at various examples across different domains:

Speech Recognition AI (like Siri, Alexa, Google Assistant): These systems are remarkably good at converting spoken words into text. They've learned to recognize phonemes, understand different accents, filter out background noise, and deal with the messiness of human speech. They're specialists in speech recognition.

But the speech recognition component itself cannot understand what the words mean, cannot respond to questions, and cannot control smart home devices. Those are separate narrow AI systems working together. The speech recognition AI does only one thing: convert audio to text.

Image Recognition AI: Systems trained to identify objects in photographs can be astonishingly accurate. They can distinguish hundreds of dog breeds, identify thousands of plant species, or detect tumors in medical images with accuracy matching or exceeding human experts.

But an AI trained to identify dog breeds cannot identify plant species without being retrained on plant data. An AI that recognizes tumors in lung scans cannot recognize tumors in brain scans without additional training. Each is a specialist in its narrow domain.

Language Translation AI: Google Translate and similar services use AI that has learned to translate between languages. These systems have studied millions of translated documents and learned patterns in how meaning is expressed differently across languages.

But translation AI cannot write original, creative content. It cannot truly understand the cultural context of what it's translating (though it gets better at this with more training). It cannot speak the languages audibly (that would require a separate speech synthesis AI). It's specialized in translation.

Recommendation AI: Netflix's recommendation system knows what movies you might like. Spotify's algorithm knows what songs match your taste. Amazon knows what products to suggest. These systems are highly specialized at predicting your preferences within their specific domain.

But Netflix's AI cannot recommend restaurants. Spotify's AI cannot recommend movies. Amazon's AI cannot generate music playlists. Each is specialized for its particular recommendation domain.

Game-Playing AI: AlphaGo, the AI that defeated the world champion at Go (a complex board game), represents a remarkable achievement. Go is far more complex than chess, with more possible positions than atoms in the universe. AlphaGo's victory demonstrated impressive pattern recognition and strategic planning.

But AlphaGo, despite its sophistication, cannot play chess, poker, or video games. It cannot recognize images. It cannot understand language. Its intelligence is entirely specialized for Go. (Though DeepMind, the company that created it, has developed other AIs for other games—each is still narrow and specific.)

Autonomous Driving AI: Self-driving car systems use AI to process sensor data, recognize objects (pedestrians, other vehicles, traffic signs), predict movement, and plan paths. This requires integrating multiple narrow AI systems.

But this AI cannot fly a plane. It cannot pilot a boat. It cannot even necessarily drive well on roads it wasn't trained on or in conditions drastically different from its training data. Its capabilities are specific to the driving task it was designed for.

The Hidden Narrowness in Seemingly Broad Systems

Some AI systems seem broader than they are because they handle what appear to be diverse tasks. Modern large language models like ChatGPT, Claude, or GPT-4 can write essays, answer questions, write code, analyze data, and engage in conversation about virtually any topic. This might seem like general intelligence, but it's still narrow AI—it's just narrow in a different way.

These systems are specifically trained on predicting text. They've learned patterns in language from enormous amounts of written text and can generate new text following those patterns. This single capability—sophisticated language pattern matching and generation—happens to be useful for many tasks that involve text.

But these systems still have crucial limitations that reveal their narrowness:

- They cannot actually manipulate physical objects or move through the world.
- They cannot form genuine intentions or goals beyond the conversation at hand.
- They cannot truly learn from individual conversations (each conversation starts fresh, though some have memory features).
- They cannot perceive the world directly through senses.
- They struggle with tasks requiring real-world common sense.
- They cannot reliably perform precise logical reasoning without errors.
- They don't truly understand causation or physical laws.

They're extraordinarily capable within the domain of language but remain narrow AI specialized in text generation, not general intelligence.

Why Narrow AI Is Narrow: Training for Specific Tasks

The narrowness of AI systems comes from how they're created. Each narrow AI is trained on specific data for a specific task, and it learns patterns relevant to that task. The training process optimizes the AI for one objective, and the resulting system embodies that optimization.

When you train an image recognition AI on pictures of cats and dogs, it learns features that distinguish cats from dogs in images. Those learned features are specifically useful for that visual classification task. They don't transfer to playing games, understanding language, or any other domain.

The AI's "intelligence" is encoded in millions or billions of numerical parameters that were adjusted during training to minimize errors on its specific task. Those parameters represent patterns specific to that task. Using them for a different task would be like trying to use a bridge blueprint to build an airplane—the detailed specifications are entirely wrong for the new purpose.

The Impressive Capabilities and Surprising Limitations of Narrow AI

What's fascinating about narrow AI is how it can simultaneously be superhuman in its domain and utterly helpless outside it. This creates some surprising contrasts:

Superhuman at Specific Tasks:

- Chess AI can defeat any human player.
- Image recognition AI can identify objects in photos more accurately than humans in many cases.
- Certain medical AI can detect diseases in scans better than experienced radiologists.
- AI can process and analyze data at scales impossible for humans.

Helpless at Adjacent Tasks:

- The chess AI cannot play a related game like checkers.
- The image recognition AI cannot describe why an image is beautiful or emotionally impactful.
- The medical AI cannot diagnose based on patient conversation or physical examination.
- The data analysis AI cannot explain its findings in accessible language without a separate language AI.

This contrast highlights the fundamental difference between narrow and general intelligence. A human who learns chess also develops general strategic thinking applicable to business, warfare, or other domains. A human who learns to recognize images also develops understanding applicable to art appreciation, navigation, and countless other visual tasks. Humans have general intelligence that transfers across domains. Narrow AI does not.

Combining Narrow AI Systems

Much of modern AI applications involve combining multiple narrow AI systems to accomplish complex tasks. Consider a fully-featured voice assistant:

1. **Speech recognition AI** converts your spoken question to text
2. **Natural language understanding AI** interprets what you're asking
3. **Information retrieval AI** searches for the answer
4. **Ranking AI** determines the best answer to return
5. **Natural language generation AI** formulates a response in conversational language
6. **Speech synthesis AI** converts the text response to spoken audio

Each component is a narrow AI specialized in its function. Together, they create the illusion of a more general intelligence, but it's really a pipeline of specialists. If any component encounters something outside its training, the whole system can fail.

This is how most sophisticated AI applications work—multiple narrow AI systems orchestrated together. A self-driving car might integrate fifty different narrow AI systems, each handling a specific aspect of perception, prediction, planning, or control.

General AI: The Holy Grail That Doesn't Exist Yet

Now let's explore general AI—what it would mean, why it doesn't exist, and why it's so much harder than narrow AI.

What Would General AI Actually Mean?

General AI (AGI—Artificial General Intelligence) would be an AI system with human-like cognitive abilities across all domains. Here's what that would entail:

- **Flexible Learning:** A general AI could learn new skills from relatively few examples, just as humans do. You can explain a new card game to a human in five minutes, and they can play. A general AI would have this same flexible learning ability, not requiring millions of training examples for each new task.
- **Transfer Learning:** General AI could apply knowledge from one domain to another. If it learns about physics, it could apply physical reasoning to engineering problems, sports, or everyday situations. If it learns about human psychology, it could apply that understanding to writing fiction, designing user interfaces, or predicting behavior.
- **Abstract Reasoning:** General AI could reason abstractly, understanding analogies, metaphors, and general principles. It could solve problems it has never encountered before by reasoning from first principles or applying analogies to known situations.

- **Common Sense:** Perhaps most challenging, general AI would need common sense—the vast store of obvious knowledge about how the world works that humans accumulate through living. Knowing that water is wet, objects fall when dropped, people get angry when insulted, coffee is typically consumed hot—millions of facts that humans know implicitly.
- **Multi-Modal Integration:** General AI would integrate information across different modes—visual, linguistic, auditory, spatial. It would understand how a written description relates to a visual scene, how spoken words connect to actions, and how abstract concepts manifest in concrete situations.
- **Goal Setting and Planning:** General AI would be capable of setting its own goals, planning long-term strategies, and pursuing objectives across different domains and timescales.
- **Adaptation to Novel Situations:** When faced with completely new situations, general AI would adapt using creativity, reasoning, and transfer of relevant knowledge—not just pattern matching against training data.

In short, general AI would be able to do anything a human mind can do, intellectually speaking. It would be a genuine artificial mind with flexible, transferable intelligence.

Why General AI Doesn't Exist

Despite decades of effort and recent impressive advances in narrow AI, general AI remains elusive. Understanding why reveals fundamental challenges:

- **The Brittleness Problem:** Current AI systems are brittle—they work well within their training distribution but fail when faced with anything significantly different. A language AI might eloquently discuss philosophy but fail at simple physical reasoning ("If I stack a book, a laptop, and a cup, which is on top?"). This brittleness indicates missing general understanding.

- **The Transfer Problem:** AI systems cannot transfer learning the way humans do. When humans learn chess, they develop strategic thinking applicable elsewhere. When AI learns chess, it develops chess-specific pattern recognition that doesn't apply to anything else. Solving this transfer problem is fundamental to achieving general AI, and we don't yet know how.
- **The Common Sense Problem:** Encoding the millions of obvious facts humans know has proven extraordinarily difficult. Much of human knowledge is implicit—we're not consciously aware of it, so we can't easily write it down to train AI. How do you train an AI that "soft things are generally more comfortable than hard things" or "people generally prefer not to be interrupted when speaking"? Humans learn this through embodied experience living in the world.
- **The Embodiment Problem:** Humans develop intelligence through physical interaction with the world. We learn about gravity by dropping things as babies, about distance by walking, and about social dynamics through thousands of interactions. Much human intelligence is grounded in physical, embodied experience. Current AI systems lack this grounding, learning only from data, which may fundamentally limit their ability to develop a general understanding.
- **The Motivation Problem:** Humans have built-in motivations, goals, and values that guide learning and action. We're curious, we seek novelty, we want to understand, we have survival instincts. AI systems have only the objectives we give them during training. Creating genuine, flexible motivation in AI is an unsolved problem.
- **The Consciousness Question:** It's unclear whether consciousness is necessary for general intelligence. If it is, we don't know how to create artificial consciousness. If it isn't, we don't know what's missing from current systems that prevents general intelligence.
- **The Computation Problem:** The human brain contains roughly 86 billion neurons with trillions of connections, running

on about 20 watts of power. Perhaps achieving general AI requires computational architectures fundamentally different from current approaches, possibly requiring orders of magnitude more computing power, or perhaps entirely different computing paradigms.

Attempts Toward General AI

Researchers pursue several approaches toward general AI, though none have succeeded yet:

Cognitive Architectures: Some researchers try to create general AI by building cognitive architectures that mimic human mental processes—memory systems, attention mechanisms, reasoning engines, learning algorithms—integrated into unified systems. Examples include SOAR, ACT-R, and others. These have achieved interesting results but remain far from general intelligence.

Whole Brain Emulation: A radical approach is to simulate an entire human brain neuron by neuron. If successful, this would create a digital mind with human-like general intelligence. However, this approach faces enormous technical challenges—we don't fully understand how brains work, and simulating 86 billion neurons with trillions of connections requires computing power beyond current capabilities.

Scaling Up Deep Learning: Some researchers believe that general AI might emerge from simply scaling up current deep learning approaches —bigger models, more data, more computing power. Recent large language models show surprising emergent capabilities, leading some to speculate that continued scaling might eventually produce general intelligence. Others argue that fundamental architectural changes are needed, not just scale.

Hybrid Approaches: Many researchers pursue hybrid approaches combining neural networks with symbolic reasoning, knowledge bases, and other techniques. The idea is that neural networks handle pattern recognition and learning while symbolic systems handle logic and reasoning, with both integrated into a more general intelligence.

Developmental Approaches: Some researchers believe AI should develop intelligence the way children do—through embodied interaction with the world over time. This approach focuses on robotics, simulation environments, and developmental learning rather than training on static datasets.

Timeline: When Might General AI Arrive?

Predictions about when general AI might be achieved vary wildly, revealing deep uncertainty:

Optimists suggest 10-30 years, believing that scaling current approaches or combining multiple techniques will achieve general AI within our lifetimes.

Pessimists suggest 50-100+ years or more, noting that fundamental problems remain unsolved and we may need breakthroughs in our understanding of intelligence itself.

Skeptics question whether general AI is even possible, suggesting that human intelligence might involve aspects that cannot be replicated in machines, or that we fundamentally misunderstand what intelligence is.

The honest answer is: we don't know. We're not even sure what we don't know. There might be one key insight away from achieving general AI, or there might be dozens of major unsolved problems.

Why the Distinction Matters

Understanding the difference between narrow AI (which exists) and general AI (which doesn't) is crucial for several reasons:

- **Realistic Expectations:** When you hear about AI achievements, understanding they're narrow AI helps set realistic expectations. Yes, AI can do impressive things, but each system is specialized. There's no AI that can "do anything."

- **Risk Assessment:** Many concerns about AI—job displacement, algorithmic bias, privacy—relate to narrow AI that exists now. Other concerns—existential risk from superintelligence, AI with its own goals—relate to general AI that doesn't exist yet. Conflating these leads to confused discussions about AI risks.
- **Investment Decisions:** Businesses considering AI need to understand that available AI is narrow and specialized. You can't buy one AI system that solves all your problems—you need specific solutions for specific tasks.
- **Policy Development:** Governments creating AI policy need to distinguish between regulating existing narrow AI and preparing for potential future general AI. These require different approaches.
- **Understanding Progress:** When you hear about AI breakthroughs, understanding the narrow-vs-general distinction helps you assess their significance. A breakthrough in one narrow domain doesn't necessarily mean we're closer to general AI.

Other Distinctions: Additional Types of AI

Beyond the narrow vs. general distinction, there are other ways to categorize AI types:

Reactive AI vs. Memory-Based AI

- **Reactive AI** makes decisions based only on current input, with no memory of past interactions. Many game-playing AIs work this way—they evaluate the current board position without remembering previous games.
- **Memory-Based AI** incorporates past experiences into decision-making. Chatbots that remember your conversation history,

recommendation systems that track your viewing history, and learning systems that improve over time are memory-based.

All existing AI, whether reactive or memory-based, is still narrow AI. This is a different dimension of variation.

Weak AI vs. Strong AI

These terms are sometimes used synonymously with narrow and general AI, but with slightly different emphasis:

- **Weak AI** refers to systems that simulate intelligence without truly possessing it. They appear intelligent but don't genuinely understand, feel, or think.
- **Strong AI** refers to systems that would genuinely possess intelligence, consciousness, and understanding—not just simulating these qualities but actually having them.

This distinction gets philosophical. All current AI is definitely "weak" in this sense—it simulates intelligent behavior through sophisticated pattern matching but doesn't genuinely understand or think. Whether "strong AI" is even possible remains a philosophical question.

Artificial Superintelligence (ASI)

Beyond general AI lies another theoretical category: artificial superintelligence—AI that surpasses human intelligence across all domains.

If we eventually create general AI on par with human intelligence, it's possible such a system could improve itself, leading to recursive self-improvement. The AI could redesign its own algorithms, making itself smarter, which would make it better at further self-improvement, leading to an "intelligence explosion."

The result would be ASI—an intelligence far exceeding human capabilities in every domain. This is even more speculative than general AI and raises profound questions about control, safety, and the future of humanity.

Some researchers, like Nick Bostrom, consider ASI the ultimate challenge and a potential existential risk. Others consider it science fiction. But it's worth noting as a category beyond even general AI on the spectrum of AI types.

Living in the Age of Narrow AI

Understanding that all current AI is narrow helps make sense of the AI-powered world we live in:

- **Why AI Seems Inconsistent:** AI can beat world champions at chess but struggles with simple common-sense reasoning. It can identify thousands of objects in images, but misinterprets obvious situations. These inconsistencies make sense once you understand that each capability is a separate, narrow AI. There's no underlying general understanding—just collections of specialized pattern recognizers.
- **Why AI Sometimes Fails Absurdly:** Narrow AI can fail in ways that seem ridiculous to humans. A self-driving car confused by unusual road markings, a chatbot giving dangerous advice, an image recognizer fooled by patterns imperceptible to humans—these failures happen because the AI only knows its narrow domain and has no general common sense to catch obvious errors.
- **Why AI Requires So Much Training Data:** Humans can learn from a few examples because we transfer knowledge from other domains. AI requires massive training data because it's learning each task from scratch without transfer. This is a fundamental limitation of narrow AI.

- **Why AI Can't Replace Human Judgment:** Because AI lacks general intelligence, common sense, and true understanding, it can't fully replace human judgment in complex situations. AI can assist, provide information, and handle routine cases, but humans remain necessary for novel situations, ethical judgment, and cases requiring holistic understanding.
- **Why AI Is Both Amazing and Limited:** Narrow AI achieves superhuman performance in specific domains while remaining helpless elsewhere. This explains why AI is simultaneously revolutionary (transforming industries through specialized capabilities) and limited (unable to replicate general human intelligence).

The Future: Narrow AI Keeps Improving, General AI Remains Distant

For the foreseeable future, we'll continue seeing advances in narrow AI:

- More accurate recognition systems
- Better language models
- More sophisticated recommendation engines
- Improved autonomous systems
- AI tackling new specialized domains

Each advance makes narrow AI more capable within specific applications. The combined effect of many improved narrow AI systems will continue transforming technology and society.

But these advances, however impressive, don't necessarily bring us closer to general AI. We're getting better at creating specialized systems, but the challenge of general intelligence remains fundamentally different—not just a matter of scaling up narrow AI, but requiring solutions to deep, unsolved problems.

Conclusion: Understanding What AI Is and Isn't

The distinction between different types of AI—especially between narrow AI that exists and general AI that doesn't—is fundamental to understanding artificial intelligence.

Current AI is narrow: Every AI system you interact with is specialized for specific tasks. It can be brilliant within its domain and helpless outside it. This includes everything from facial recognition to language models to game-playing systems.

General AI doesn't exist: No AI system can learn flexibly across domains, transfer knowledge the way humans do, exercise common sense, or demonstrate human-like general intelligence. This capability remains a goal, not a reality.

The gap is fundamental, not incremental: Achieving general AI isn't just about making narrow AI better—it requires solving deep problems about transfer learning, common sense, flexible reasoning, and possibly consciousness.

Both types matter: Narrow AI is transforming the world right now and raises important practical questions about jobs, privacy, bias, and societal impact. General AI remains theoretical but raises profound questions about the future of intelligence and humanity's place in it.

Understanding these distinctions helps you think clearly about AI—appreciating what current systems can do, recognizing their limitations, setting realistic expectations, and engaging meaningfully in discussions about AI's present impact and future trajectory.

When someone claims "AI can do X," you can now ask: "Is that narrow AI specialized for X, or are you imagining general AI?" Almost always, the answer is narrow AI, which helps calibrate your understanding of what's actually possible versus what's speculation.

We live in an age of increasingly capable, narrow AI—specialized systems that excel at specific tasks. Whether we'll eventually create general AI that matches human flexibility remains one of the great open questions of our time. Until then, understanding the difference between these types helps us navigate the AI-powered present while thinking clearly about possible futures.

Seven
The Recent AI Boom
Understanding What's Changed and Why It Matters

What's changed recently is that AI can now generate new content—writing essays, creating images, and holding conversations. These are called "generative AI" systems, and they're trained on vast amounts of text, images, or other data from the internet.

If you've been paying attention to technology news over the past few years, you've probably noticed that AI seems to be everywhere suddenly. Terms like ChatGPT, Midjourney, DALL-E, and "generative AI" have exploded into public consciousness. Something fundamental has shifted in artificial intelligence, and it's not just hype—there's been a genuine technological breakthrough that's changing what AI can do. Let's explore exactly what's changed, why it happened now, and what it means.

Before the Boom: What AI Could Do

To understand what's changed, we need to understand what AI was like before the recent boom. For decades, AI excelled at analysis and classification but struggled with creation.

AI Was Good At Recognition and Classification:

Before around 2020, AI could analyze existing content remarkably well:

- Recognize faces in photos with high accuracy
- Identify objects in images (this is a cat, that's a car)
- Transcribe spoken words into text

- Classify emails as spam or not spam
- Translate text from one language to another
- Recommend products based on your purchase history
- Play games like chess or Go at superhuman levels

All of these tasks involve looking at something that exists and making judgments about it. The AI receives input and produces analysis, classification, or prediction. It's consuming and understanding (in a limited sense) but not creating.

AI Was Bad At Creation:

What AI struggled with was generating genuinely new, high-quality content:

- Writing coherent, meaningful text longer than a few sentences
- Creating realistic, detailed images from descriptions
- Composing original music that sounded professional
- Having natural conversations that stayed on topic
- Generating video content
- Creating art with specific styles and subjects

When AI did generate content before the boom, the results were often noticeably artificial—clunky text, distorted images, or outputs that quickly revealed themselves as machine-generated. Creative generation seemed to require something AI didn't have.

This limitation made sense to many people. Analysis seems mechanical—following patterns and rules. But creation seems to require imagination, understanding, and maybe even consciousness. How could a machine truly create something new?

The Breakthrough: Generative AI Emerges

Then, starting around 2018-2020 and accelerating dramatically in 2022-2023, something changed. A new category of AI systems emerged that could generate remarkably high-quality, original content. These are called "generative AI" systems.

What Is Generative AI?

Generative AI refers to artificial intelligence systems that can create new content—text, images, audio, video, code, and more—rather than just analyzing existing content. These systems don't just classify or predict; they generate.

The keyword is "generate." These systems produce new outputs that didn't exist before. Ask a generative AI to write a poem about robots dreaming of sheep, and it creates original text that didn't exist anywhere. Ask it to create an image of a cat wearing a spacesuit on Mars, and it generates a unique image. The content is genuinely new, not copied from somewhere.

The Major Types of Generative AI:

Several categories of generative AI have emerged:

- **Text Generation (Large Language Models):** Systems like ChatGPT, GPT-4, Claude, Google's Gemini, and others can write essays, answer questions, have conversations, write code, compose emails, create stories, and more. They generate human-like text on virtually any topic.
- **Image Generation:** Systems like DALL-E, Midjourney, Stable Diffusion, and Adobe Firefly can create images from text descriptions. Type "a serene lake at sunset with mountains in the background, oil painting style," and they generate that image.
- **Code Generation:** Tools like GitHub Copilot can write computer code based on descriptions of what you want the code to do, significantly accelerating software development.
- **Audio Generation:** Systems can now generate realistic speech

in any voice, create original music in specified styles, and even generate sound effects.
- **Video Generation:** Emerging systems like Sora and others can generate video clips from text descriptions, though this capability is still developing compared to text and image generation.

Each of these represents a fundamental expansion of what AI can do—moving from analysis to creation.

What Made This Possible: Three Key Ingredients

The generative AI boom didn't happen because of a single invention. Instead, it resulted from the convergence of three crucial elements that came together at the right time.

Ingredient 1: Massive Amounts of Training Data

Generative AI systems learn by studying enormous amounts of existing content. The internet provided an unprecedented data source.

For Text Generation: Language models are trained on vast text datasets scraped from the internet—books, articles, websites, forums, social media, code repositories, and more. GPT-3, for example, was trained on hundreds of billions of words. GPT-4 and similar models are used even more.

This massive text corpus contains countless examples of:

- How sentences are structured
- How ideas connect
- How different topics are discussed
- How conversations flow
- How stories are told
- How arguments are constructed
- How code is written

- How facts relate to each other

By studying these billions of examples, the AI learns patterns in human language—not just grammar and vocabulary, but the deeper structures of how humans communicate meaning through text.

For Image Generation: Image generation systems are trained on hundreds of millions or billions of images paired with text descriptions. These datasets include:

- Photographs with captions
- Artwork with titles and descriptions
- Product images with labels
- Scientific images with annotations

The AI learns relationships between text descriptions and visual content. It learns that "sunset" correlates with orange and red hues in the sky, that "cat" correlates with certain shapes and features, and that "oil painting" correlates with particular textures and styles.

Why This Much Data Matters:

Previous AI systems were trained on thousands or maybe millions of examples. Generative AI uses billions. This scale makes a qualitative difference. With enough examples, the AI can learn subtle patterns, handle rare situations, and generate content that feels natural and diverse rather than repetitive or formulaic.

The internet made this scale possible. Thirty years ago, gathering billions of text examples or millions of labeled images would have been impossible. But the internet contains exabytes of text and images, providing training data at a scale previously unimaginable.

Ingredient 2: Powerful Computing Resources

Training generative AI requires enormous computational power—far more than earlier AI systems.

The Hardware: Modern AI training relies heavily on specialized chips called GPUs (Graphics Processing Units) and TPUs (Tensor Processing Units). These chips can perform thousands of mathematical operations simultaneously, making them ideal for the parallel computations AI training requires.

A single large language model might be trained using thousands of these chips running continuously for weeks or months. The electricity cost alone can reach millions of dollars. Companies like OpenAI, Google, Meta, and others have invested in massive computing infrastructure specifically for AI training.

Why So Much Computation?

Generative AI models are enormous. GPT-3 has 175 billion parameters—individual numbers that the system adjusts during training. GPT-4 and similar models are even larger, with estimates suggesting over a trillion parameters.

Processing billions of training examples through models with hundreds of billions of parameters requires astronomical amounts of computation. Each training example requires billions of mathematical operations. Multiply that by billions of examples, repeated many times over, and you're talking about computations that would take a single computer thousands of years. But with thousands of specialized chips working in parallel, it becomes feasible in weeks or months.

The Cost Barrier:

This computational requirement creates a significant barrier. Only organizations with substantial resources—major tech companies and well-funded startups—can train the largest, most capable generative AI models from scratch. This has implications for who controls this technology and how it develops.

However, once trained, these models can be used (called "inference") with much less computational power, making them accessible to everyday users through cloud services.

Ingredient 3: Architectural Innovations (Transformers)

Having lots of data and computing power isn't enough—you need the right algorithm to make use of them. The key architectural innovation was the "transformer" architecture, introduced in 2017.

What Are Transformers?

Without getting too technical, transformers are a way of structuring neural networks that's particularly effective for processing sequences (like sentences) and understanding relationships between different parts of the input.

The key innovation is something called "attention mechanisms." These allow the AI to focus on relevant parts of the input when processing each element. When reading a sentence, the transformer can "pay attention" to earlier words that provide context for understanding later words.

For example, in the sentence "The trophy didn't fit in the suitcase because it was too big," a transformer can determine that "it" refers to the trophy (not the suitcase) by attending to the relationships between all the words. This ability to handle long-range dependencies and context is crucial for generating coherent text.

Why Transformers Work So Well:

Transformers scale effectively—they get better with more data and more computing power, unlike earlier architectures. This scalability is why they've been so successful for generative AI.

They're also versatile—the same basic architecture works for text, images, audio, and other types of data with appropriate modifications. This has led to rapid progress across multiple domains.

The Progression:

The transformer architecture was introduced in 2017 with a paper titled "Attention Is All You Need." It was initially used for language translation. Then:

- 2018: BERT (from Google) used transformers for language understanding
- 2018-2019: GPT-1 and GPT-2 (from OpenAI) used transformers for text generation
- 2020: GPT-3 scaled up transformers dramatically, showing surprising capabilities
- 2021-2022: DALL-E and similar systems applied transformer concepts to image generation
- 2022-2023: ChatGPT and GPT-4 brought transformer-based generative AI to mainstream attention

Each step demonstrated that scaling up transformer-based models with more data and computing power continued to improve performance, encouraging further investment and development.

The Moment Everything Changed: ChatGPT's Launch

While the underlying technology had been developing for years, generative AI burst into public consciousness with the launch of ChatGPT in November 2022.

Why ChatGPT Was Different:

ChatGPT wasn't the first large language model—GPT-3 had been available through an API since 2020, and other companies had similar systems. But ChatGPT was the first to be packaged in a way that made its capabilities obvious and accessible to everyone:

- **Free and easy to use:** Anyone could try it without technical knowledge or payment
- **Conversational interface:** The chat format felt natural and approachable
- **Impressive capabilities:** It could write essays, debug code, explain concepts, and more
- **Surprising versatility:** It handled an enormous range of tasks people threw at it

Within days, millions of people were experimenting with ChatGPT, sharing examples of what it could do, and being genuinely amazed. It felt like a glimpse of the future.

The Viral Moment:

ChatGPT reached 1 million users in just five days—faster than any consumer application in history. Within two months, it had over 100 million users. Social media is filled with examples:

- Students using it to write essays
- Programmers using it to debug code
- Writers using it to brainstorm ideas
- People having philosophical conversations with it
- Teachers concerned about cheating
- Businesses exploring applications

This viral moment created intense public awareness of and interest in AI. Suddenly, everyone was talking about AI, not just technology enthusiasts.

The Competitive Response:

ChatGPT's success triggered a competitive frenzy in the tech industry:

- Google rushed to release Bard (now Gemini), its conversational AI
- Microsoft invested billions in OpenAI and integrated GPT into Bing and Office
- Meta released LLaMA, an open-source language model
- Anthropic (where I come from) released Claude
- Countless startups launched products built on generative AI
- Every major tech company announced AI initiatives

This competition accelerated development, with new, more capable models released every few months.

What Makes Generative AI Different: Why It Feels Revolutionary

Generative AI feels qualitatively different from previous AI because of several unique characteristics:

It Creates Rather Than Analyzes

Previous AI systems were impressive but fundamentally reactive—they analyzed, classified, or predicted based on what you showed them. Generative AI is proactive—it creates something new based on what you ask for.

This shift feels profound because creation has always been distinctly human. We've grown accustomed to machines calculating, sorting, and processing, but machines that write poetry, paint pictures, and compose music challenge our sense of what makes humans special.

It Handles Open-Ended Tasks

Earlier AI systems excelled at narrow, well-defined tasks: "Is this email spam?" "What object is in this image?" "What's the best chess move?" These have clear answers.

Generative AI handles open-ended requests: "Write a story about a robot learning to love." "Create an image of hope." "Explain quantum physics to a child." These don't have single correct answers, yet the AI produces reasonable, often impressive responses.

This open-endedness makes generative AI feel more intelligent and versatile—more like a capable assistant than a specialized tool.

It Uses Natural Language

You interact with generative AI using regular human language, not technical commands or forms. You just describe what you want in plain English (or other languages), and it understands.

This natural language interface is revolutionary because it makes AI accessible to everyone. You don't need to learn programming or understand technical specifications. If you can describe what you want, the AI can try to create it.

This drastically lowers the barrier to using AI, democratizing access to powerful capabilities.

It Seems to Understand Context

Generative AI appears to understand context and nuance in ways earlier systems didn't. You can have multi-turn conversations where the AI remembers what you discussed earlier. You can give complex, nuanced instructions, and it follows them.

For example, you might say: "Write a story about a detective, but make it funny rather than serious, set it in the 1920s, and include a twist ending where the detective was actually wrong all along." Earlier AI couldn't parse such complex, multifaceted instructions. Generative AI handles them smoothly.

This apparent contextual understanding makes interactions feel more natural and intelligent.

It Displays Emergent Abilities

Perhaps most surprising, large generative AI models display "emergent abilities"—capabilities that emerge at scale that weren't explicitly trained for.

For example, large language models can:

- Solve math problems by reasoning through them step-by-step

- Translate between languages that they weren't specifically trained to translate
- Write computer code in programming languages not emphasized in training
- Understand and create humor, metaphors, and analogies

These abilities weren't explicitly programmed—they emerged from the general pattern-learning process at a sufficient scale. This suggests that something qualitatively different happens when you train large enough models on enough data, though researchers don't fully understand why.

The Explosion of Applications

The capabilities of generative AI have led to an explosion of applications across virtually every domain:

Writing and Content Creation

Professional Writing: Journalists use AI to draft initial article structures, writers use it to overcome writer's block, marketers use it to generate ad copy, and businesses use it to create reports.

Creative Writing: Authors experiment with AI for brainstorming plot ideas, generating character descriptions, or writing entire stories. Some published books now acknowledge AI assistance.

Email and Communication: Many professionals use AI to draft emails, summarize long threads, or translate messages into different tones (more formal, friendlier, more concise).

Educational Content: Teachers use AI to create lesson plans, generate quiz questions, and explain concepts in different ways. Students use it for research and understanding difficult topics (though concerns about cheating remain).

Visual Arts and Design

Digital Art: Artists use image generation AI for concept art, illustration, texture creation, and inspiration. Some create art entirely with AI, others use it as one tool among many.

Graphic Design: Designers generate logos, marketing materials, product mockups, and design variations much faster than traditional methods allowed.

Photography and Editing: AI can enhance photos, remove unwanted elements, change backgrounds, or generate entirely synthetic photographs indistinguishable from real ones.

Architecture and Product Design: Designers generate visualizations of buildings, interiors, or products from descriptions, accelerating the ideation phase.

Software Development

Code Generation: Programmers use AI to write boilerplate code, implement standard functions, convert code between languages, and generate entire applications from descriptions.

Debugging: AI helps identify bugs, suggest fixes, and explain why code isn't working.

Documentation: AI generates code comments, documentation, and explains what existing code does.

Learning: People learning programming use AI as an always-available tutor that explains concepts and answers questions.

Business and Productivity

Customer Service: AI-powered chatbots handle customer inquiries, troubleshoot problems, and route complex issues to humans.

Data Analysis: AI helps analyze business data, generate reports, and identify patterns or insights.

Meeting Summaries: AI transcribes meetings and generates summaries with action items.

Research: Professionals use AI to synthesize information from multiple sources, answer research questions, and draft literature reviews.

Education and Learning

Tutoring: AI provides personalized tutoring, explaining concepts in different ways until students understand.

Language Learning: AI conversation partners help practice foreign languages with infinite patience.

Study Aids: AI generates practice problems, creates study guides, and quizzes students on material.

Accessibility: AI makes education more accessible by translating content, creating alternative formats, and adapting to different learning styles.

Entertainment and Media

Gaming: AI generates game content, creates character dialogue, and even designs entire game levels.

Music: AI composes original music in specified styles, generates background music, or creates variations on themes.

Video: Emerging AI systems generate video content, create special effects, and even generate synthetic actors.

Healthcare

Medical Writing: AI helps doctors write patient notes, summarize medical records, and generate reports.

Patient Communication: AI drafts patient communication in understandable language and answers common medical questions.

Research: Medical researchers use AI to analyze literature, generate hypotheses, and write research papers.

Drug Discovery: AI helps design new molecules and predict which compounds might make effective drugs.

The Controversies and Concerns

The rapid rise of generative AI has sparked significant controversies and concerns:

Copyright and Training Data

Generative AI is trained on vast amounts of content from the internet—text, images, music, and code. Much of this content is copyrighted. This raises questions:

- Is it legal to train AI on copyrighted material without permission?
- If AI generates content similar to copyrighted works, is that infringement?
- Should creators be compensated when their work trains AI?

Multiple lawsuits are currently addressing these questions, and the legal landscape remains unsettled. Some argue that AI training is "fair use" similar to how humans learn from existing art. Others argue it's mass copyright violation on an unprecedented scale.

Job Displacement

If AI can write, create art, code, and perform many cognitive tasks, what happens to people whose jobs involve these activities?

Concerns exist for:

- Writers and journalists
- Artists and illustrators
- Programmers
- Customer service representatives
- Translators
- Tutors and educators

Some argue AI will eliminate jobs, while others argue it will augment human capabilities, making people more productive rather than replacing them. The reality is likely complex, with some jobs displaced, others transformed, and new jobs created.

Misinformation and Fake Content

Generative AI makes it trivially easy to create:

- Fake news articles that appear legitimate
- Fake images of events that never happened
- Fake videos of people saying things they never said ("deepfakes")
- Fake social media accounts with AI-generated content
- Sophisticated phishing emails and scams

This capability threatens to flood the internet with synthetic content, making it increasingly difficult to distinguish real from fake. This has implications for political discourse, journalism, trust in information, and potentially legal evidence.

Education and Academic Integrity

Students can use AI to write essays, solve homework problems, and complete assignments. This challenges educational systems built around evaluating students through such assignments.

Questions arise:

- How do we assess learning if AI can complete traditional assignments?
- Should students be allowed to use AI? If so, how much?
- How do we detect AI-generated work?
- Do we need to fundamentally rethink assessment methods?

Bias and Fairness

Generative AI learns from internet data, which reflects human biases—racial, gender, cultural, and others. The AI can perpetuate or even amplify these biases:

- Generating stereotypical images (e.g., showing CEOs as mostly male and white)
- Providing biased advice or information
- Using language that reflects cultural biases
- Making unfair assumptions about people

Addressing these biases is an active area of research, but it remains challenging because the biases are embedded in the training data that represents human culture and history.

Privacy

If generative AI is trained on internet data, it might have learned from:

- Personal information that was publicly posted
- Private information that was leaked or hacked
- Copyrighted personal works

There are concerns about AI revealing personal information it learned from training data, generating realistic fake content about real people, and potential privacy violations in how training data was collected.

Existential Concerns

Some researchers worry that continued AI advancement could eventually pose existential risks if AI systems become more capable than humans and pursue goals misaligned with human values. While generative AI today doesn't pose such risks, some see it as a step toward more advanced AI that might.

Why Now? What Triggered the Boom at This Moment?

Given that the key ingredients (transformers, big data, computing power) had been developing for years, why did the boom happen in 2022-2023 specifically?

Crossing a Capability Threshold

AI capabilities had been improving gradually, but somewhere around 2022, they crossed a threshold where the outputs became consistently good enough to be genuinely useful rather than just interesting experiments.

Earlier systems were impressive in demos but frustrating in practice—they'd generate text that started well but devolved into nonsense, or images that were obviously flawed. Recent systems generate outputs that are reliably good enough for practical use. This reliability threshold is crucial for mainstream adoption.

The Accessibility Moment (ChatGPT)

As discussed earlier, ChatGPT made generative AI accessible and understandable to the general public for the first time. This created awareness, excitement, and demand that accelerated everything.

Investment and Competition

Once ChatGPT demonstrated market potential, investment flooded into AI. Microsoft invested $10 billion in OpenAI, Google accelerated its AI efforts, and countless startups received funding. This money accelerated development, creating a positive feedback loop.

Improved Training Techniques

Beyond just scale, researchers developed better training techniques:

- RLHF (Reinforcement Learning from Human Feedback) made AI systems better at following instructions and being helpful.
- Better data curation improved training data quality.
- Improved architectures made models more efficient.
- Fine-tuning techniques adapted general models for specific uses.

These refinements made the difference between "impressive in research labs" and "useful for millions of people."

Cultural Readiness

After years of hearing about AI in science fiction and gradual AI improvements in everyday products, the public was primed to recognize and appreciate generative AI when it arrived. The ground had been prepared for a breakthrough to capture attention.

What's Next: Where Is Generative AI Heading?

The generative AI boom is ongoing, with rapid developments continuing:

- **Multimodal Models**

Current systems typically handle one type of content—text or images, or audio. The next generation combines multiple modalities in single models (understanding images and describing them in text, generating images from text descriptions, understanding and generating audio, processing video).

These multimodal systems will be more versatile and capable.

- **Longer Context**

Current systems can process limited amounts of text at once (though this limit keeps increasing). Future systems will handle much longer contexts —entire books, long conversations, extensive documents—making them more useful for complex tasks.

- **Better Reasoning**

Current generative AI sometimes makes logical errors or fails at multi-step reasoning. Significant effort is going into improving reasoning capabilities, making AI better at mathematics, logic, planning, and complex problem-solving.

- **Personalization**

Future systems will better adapt to individual users—learning your preferences, remembering your previous interactions, and tailoring responses to your needs while respecting privacy.

- **Specialized Models**

While general-purpose models are impressive, specialized models trained for specific domains (medicine, law, engineering, etc.) will likely offer superior performance in those areas.

- **Reduced Costs**

As techniques improve and computing becomes more efficient, the cost of using generative AI will decrease, making it accessible for more applications and users.

- **Integration Everywhere**

Generative AI will be integrated into most software products—word processors, design tools, programming environments, email clients, and countless other applications—as a standard feature rather than a standalone product.

Conclusion: We're Living Through a Technological Inflection Point

The recent AI boom represents a genuine technological breakthrough, not just hype. For the first time, AI can generate new, high-quality content across multiple domains—text, images, code, and more. This capability emerged from the convergence of three key factors: massive training data from the internet, enormous computing resources, and innovative transformer architectures.

What's Different: Unlike previous AI that analyzed and classified, generative AI creates. It handles open-ended tasks using natural language, making it accessible to everyone. It displays emergent abilities that weren't explicitly programmed, suggesting qualitatively new capabilities.

Why Now: The boom happened when capabilities crossed a threshold from "interesting" to "useful," when ChatGPT made these capabilities accessible and obvious, and when massive investment accelerated development into a competitive race.

The Impact: Generative AI is already transforming content creation, software development, customer service, education, and countless other domains. It's creating new opportunities while raising concerns about copyright, jobs, misinformation, and bias.

Looking Ahead: The technology continues to develop rapidly. Models are becoming more capable, multimodal, better at reasoning, and more widely integrated. We're likely in the early stages of understanding how generative AI will reshape work, creativity, and society.

The generative AI boom isn't a bubble or temporary fad—it's a fundamental expansion of what AI can do, made possible by specific technological achievements that came together at this moment in history. We're living through an inflection point in how humans interact with technology and how creative and cognitive work gets done.

Whether this fills you with excitement or concern likely depends on your perspective, but one thing is clear: the recent changes in AI capabilities are real, significant, and will have lasting effects on technology and society. Understanding what's changed and why helps us navigate this transformation more thoughtfully and prepare for what comes next.

Eight
AI Has Real Limitations
Understanding What Machines Can't Do

AI doesn't truly "understand" things the way you do. It can write about Paris without knowing what the Eiffel Tower actually looks like in person. It makes mistakes, can be confidently wrong, and struggles with things kids find easy, like common sense.

In all the excitement about what AI can do—writing essays, creating art, answering questions, and seemingly demonstrating intelligence—it's crucial to understand what AI cannot do. Despite impressive capabilities, AI has fundamental limitations that distinguish it from human intelligence. Understanding these limitations helps us use AI appropriately, recognize its mistakes, and appreciate what makes human intelligence special.

The Fundamental Limitation: AI Doesn't Truly Understand

The most important limitation of AI is also the most difficult to grasp: AI doesn't understand things the way humans do. This sounds simple, but its implications are profound and far-reaching.

What Does "Understanding" Mean?

When you understand something, you grasp its meaning, its connections to other things, its implications, and its significance. Understanding involves:

Conceptual Grasp: When you understand what a "chair" is, you don't just recognize chair-shaped objects. You understand that chairs are for sitting, that they're furniture, that they serve a purpose, that they're designed by humans, that different cultures have different chair styles, that you'd look for one when tired, and countless other connections.

Contextual Knowledge: You understand that mentioning "sitting down" in a conversation might be suggesting taking a break, showing hospitality, or preparing for a serious discussion. You grasp the social and emotional contexts, not just the literal meaning.

Causal Understanding: You understand that if you pull a chair out from under someone, they'll fall. You understand why—because chairs support weight, people need support to sit, and removing support causes falling. You grasp the physical causation.

Experiential Foundation: Your understanding of chairs is grounded in experience. You've sat in chairs, felt their support, experienced comfort or discomfort, moved chairs around, and physically interacted with them thousands of times. This embodied experience gives meaning depth.

Flexible Application: Because you truly understand chairs, you can answer novel questions: "Could a chair be used as a weapon?" "Would a chair work on the moon?" "Could you make a chair from ice?" You can reason about chairs in contexts you've never encountered because you understand the underlying concepts.

What AI Has Instead of Understanding

AI doesn't have this rich sense of understanding. What it has instead is statistical pattern recognition—incredibly sophisticated, but fundamentally different from understanding.

Pattern Matching: When an AI processes the word "chair," it has learned statistical associations. It knows that "chair" often appears near words like "sit," "table," "furniture," "wood," and "comfortable" in its training data. It has mathematical representations encoding these associations.

The AI can generate sensible-sounding text about chairs because it has learned patterns in how humans write about chairs. But it hasn't sat in a chair, doesn't know what sitting feels like, and doesn't grasp the purpose or function of chairs except as linguistic patterns.

No Grounding in Reality: AI learns from text and images, but these are representations of reality, not reality itself. An AI can process millions of sentences about water being wet, but it has never experienced wetness. It knows the word "wet" appears in certain contexts, but it doesn't know what wetness is.

This lack of grounding means the AI's "knowledge" is fundamentally different from yours. You know what wet means because you've experienced it. The AI knows wet as a pattern in language data.

No Causal Models: When you drop a glass and it breaks, you understand the causal chain: gravity pulled it down, it hit the floor with force, glass is brittle, impact exceeds glass strength, therefore it shatters. You have a mental model of physical causation.

AI doesn't have such models. It might predict that "The glass fell and broke" is a likely sentence completion because it's seen similar sentences, but it doesn't understand the physics of why glasses break when dropped.

No Goals or Intentions: When you write a sentence, you have intentions—you want to communicate something, persuade someone, request information, or express emotion. You're pursuing goals.

AI generates text by predicting what words are likely to follow previous words based on patterns in training data. It's not trying to communicate anything to anyone. It has no desires, goals, or intentions. The text it produces is a sophisticated pattern-following, not intentional communication.

The Paris Example: Knowledge Without Experience

The example about Paris perfectly illustrates this limitation. An AI can write eloquently about Paris:

> *"Paris, the City of Light, captivates visitors with its elegant boulevards and iconic landmarks. The Eiffel Tower dominates the skyline, its iron latticework a marvel of 19th-century engineering. The Seine winds through the city, its banks lined with historic buildings and charming bookstalls. Cafés spill onto sidewalks where locals and tourists alike savor coffee and conversation."*

This sounds knowledgeable and evocative. The AI has generated text that humans would recognize as being about Paris, incorporating correct facts and appropriate descriptions.

But the AI has never seen Paris. It has never experienced the moment of rounding a corner and suddenly seeing the Eiffel Tower looming above. It doesn't know the feeling of walking along the Seine on a spring evening or the smell of fresh croissants from a bakery. It has never navigated Paris's Metro system or felt lost in Montmartre's winding streets.

What the AI Actually Did: The AI processed millions of texts about Paris during training. It learned statistical patterns:

- "Paris" is strongly associated with "Eiffel Tower," "Seine," "France," and "capital."
- Descriptions of Paris frequently include words like "romantic," "historic," and "elegant."
- Certain phrases commonly appear together: "City of Light," "iron latticework," "charming cafés."

When asked to write about Paris, the AI generates text following these learned patterns. The result sounds knowledgeable because it reflects patterns found in human-written texts about Paris. But there's no actual knowledge or understanding behind it—just pattern recognition and generation.

Why This Matters: A human who's been to Paris writes from experience and memory. They might describe a specific moment, a personal reaction, an unexpected detail. Their writing is grounded in reality.

The AI's writing, however beautiful, is untethered from reality. It's a simulation of knowledge based on linguistic patterns. This becomes problematic when the patterns in training data are wrong, incomplete, or misleading—the AI has no way to know because it lacks grounding in actual experience.

Limitation: AI Makes Mistakes

AI systems make mistakes, sometimes simple ones that seem inexplicable given their impressive capabilities in other areas.

Types of Mistakes AI Makes

Factual Errors: AI sometimes states incorrect facts with complete confidence. It might say a historical event happened in the wrong year, attribute a quote to the wrong person, or claim a scientific fact that's false.

These errors occur because the AI learned patterns from training data that included errors, or because it's predicting what words are likely rather than retrieving verified facts. It's generating text based on statistical patterns, not consulting an accurate knowledge base.

Logical Inconsistencies: AI might contradict itself within a single response, especially in longer outputs. It might state something in one paragraph and say the opposite a few paragraphs later, not realizing the contradiction because it's not tracking logical consistency—it's predicting likely next words based on recent context.

Mathematical Errors: Despite being computers, AI systems sometimes make arithmetic mistakes when generating text. They might say "15 + 7 = 21" because they're predicting digits that commonly appear after "15 + 7 =" in training data, not because they're actually calculating.

Some AI systems have access to calculators or code execution to compensate for this weakness, but the underlying language model itself isn't performing calculations—it's pattern matching.

Nonsensical Outputs: Sometimes AI generates text that's grammatically correct but meaningless or absurd: "The colorless green ideas slept furiously" is grammatically valid but nonsensical. AI can produce similar output when patterns in training data lead it astray.

Context Loss: In longer conversations or documents, AI may lose track of earlier context, forgetting important constraints or information mentioned earlier. This happens because the AI's "memory" is limited—it can only consider a certain amount of recent text when generating its next output.

The "Hallucination" Problem

A particularly significant issue is AI "hallucination"—when AI confidently generates false information that sounds plausible.

Why Hallucinations Happen: AI is fundamentally a prediction system. When asked a question, it predicts what a good answer would look like based on patterns in training data. If it doesn't actually know the answer, it might generate something that fits the pattern of what answers look like, even if the content is false.

For example, if you ask an AI for recent news, it might generate plausible-sounding but entirely fabricated news stories because it's learned the pattern of how news stories are structured and written, but it doesn't have actual current information.

Legal Case Example: There have been cases where lawyers used AI to help write legal briefs, and the AI cited court cases that didn't exist. The

AI generated case names and citations that looked correct—following the pattern of how legal citations are formatted—but the cases were completely fictional.

The lawyers didn't catch these errors and submitted briefs with fake citations, leading to professional consequences. This illustrates the danger of AI's confident-sounding but potentially false outputs.

Why It's Dangerous: Hallucinations are particularly problematic because:

- The false information sounds plausible and authoritative.
- There's no indication that the AI is uncertain or guessing.
- Users might trust the output without verification.
- The errors can be subtle and difficult to spot.

This means AI output always requires human verification, especially for important uses.

The Confidence Problem

Perhaps most concerning, AI displays no correlation between confidence and correctness. It states incorrect information with the same confident tone as correct information.

Humans Show Uncertainty: When humans are uncertain, we usually signal it: "I think it might be..." "If I remember correctly..." "I'm not sure, but..." These verbal cues help listeners calibrate how much to trust what we're saying.

AI Lacks Calibrated Confidence: AI generates text by predicting what's likely to come next, but this prediction confidence doesn't necessarily reflect whether the content is actually true. The AI might be very confident (in the statistical sense) about what words to generate while being completely wrong about the facts.

Most AI systems don't naturally express uncertainty. They'll state "The capital of Australia is Sydney" (wrong—it's Canberra) with the same confident tone as "The capital of France is Paris" (correct).

Some newer AI systems are being trained to better express uncertainty and avoid claiming knowledge they don't have, but this remains an active challenge.

Limitation: AI Lacks Common Sense

Common sense—the basic understanding of how the world works that humans acquire through living—is something AI notably lacks. This absence leads to failures that seem absurd given AI's sophistication in other areas.

What Is Common Sense?

Common sense is the collection of intuitive knowledge about the world that humans take for granted:

Physical Common Sense:

- Objects fall down, not up
- Solid objects can't pass through each other
- Things farther away look smaller
- Wet things eventually dry
- Heavy things are harder to lift than light things
- You can't fit a large object inside a smaller container

Social Common Sense:

- People get upset when insulted
- Smiling usually indicates happiness or friendliness
- It's rude to interrupt someone mid-sentence
- People need food and sleep
- Children are smaller than adults

- Giving gifts is often a friendly gesture

Temporal Common Sense:

- The past can't be changed
- Future events haven't happened yet
- Cause precedes effect
- Things don't spontaneously appear or disappear
- Time moves in one direction

Practical Common Sense:

- If you're cold, putting on a sweater helps
- You can't use a broken tool effectively
- Roads are for traveling between places
- Keys unlock doors
- Food expires and can become unsafe

Humans acquire this knowledge through years of living, observing, and interacting with the world. By age five, children have absorbed enormous amounts of common-sense knowledge without anyone explicitly teaching them.

Why AI Lacks Common Sense

No Embodied Experience: AI learns from text and images, not from living in and interacting with the physical world. It has never felt gravity, experienced temperature, manipulated objects, or moved through space. This lack of embodied experience means it doesn't naturally develop intuitions about physical reality.

Text-Only Learning: Most of what AI learns comes from text—written descriptions of the world. But much common-sense knowledge is never written down because it's too obvious. No one writes "water is wet" or "rocks are hard" in most texts because everyone already knows it.

The knowledge that is written tends to be the interesting, unusual, or explicitly educational content—not the mundane, obvious facts that constitute common sense.

No Survival Pressure: Humans develop common sense partly because our survival depends on understanding the world. A child learns that hot things burn through painful experience. We learn what's safe and what's dangerous through consequences.

AI has no survival needs, no pain, no physical consequences. It's just predicting text based on patterns. There's no evolutionary or experiential pressure to develop accurate models of physical reality.

Statistical Quirks: Sometimes statistical patterns in training data contradict common sense. If unusual scenarios are discussed more often than ordinary ones in text, the AI might learn biased patterns. Stories about dogs that can't swim (unusual) might be written about more than dogs that can swim (ordinary), potentially confusing the AI about typical dog capabilities.

Examples of Common-Sense Failures

AI's lack of common sense produces some notable failures:

- **Physical Reasoning Failure:** Asked "If I stack a book, then a laptop, then a cup, which one is on top?" An AI might struggle because it's doing linguistic pattern matching rather than spatial reasoning. A five-year-old easily understands this because they have physical experience with stacking.
- **Temporal Reasoning Failure:** Given "John went to the store and bought milk. Before he went to the store, he ate breakfast," an AI might sometimes get confused about the order of events, despite "before" being explicitly stated, because it's matching patterns rather than tracking temporal logic.

- **Practical Reasoning Failure:** Asked "Why can't you use a broken hammer to drive in nails?", an AI might generate various answers, but it doesn't viscerally understand the problem the way someone who's tried using a broken tool does. Its knowledge is theoretical, from patterns in text, not grounded in practical experience.
- **Social Reasoning Failure:** An AI might not understand why "I love your terrible haircut" is insulting despite containing the word "love." The sarcasm, social context, and human understanding of insults require social common sense that AI lacks.
- **Absurd Scenarios:** AI might treat absurd scenarios as reasonable because it lacks common sense to recognize absurdity. Asked "How many elephants can fit in a teaspoon?", it might attempt to calculate this mathematically rather than recognizing the question as nonsensical.

The Winograd Schema Challenge

Researchers created the "Winograd Schema Challenge" specifically to test common-sense reasoning. These are sentences with ambiguous pronouns that humans resolve easily using common sense, but machines find difficult:

"The trophy doesn't fit in the suitcase because it's too big." What is too big? (The trophy)

"The trophy doesn't fit in the suitcase because it's too small." What is too small? (The suitcase)

Humans instantly understand these through common-sense knowledge of physical objects and spatial relationships. AI must rely on statistical patterns in language, making it more prone to errors.

While modern large language models perform better on these tasks than earlier AI, they still sometimes fail, revealing gaps in genuine common-sense understanding.

Limitation: AI Struggles With Novel Situations

Another significant limitation is AI's difficulty with truly novel situations—scenarios substantially different from its training data.

The Training Data Boundary

AI can only work well within the boundaries of what it's been trained on. When faced with situations outside its training data distribution, performance degrades.

Recognition Example: An image recognition AI trained primarily on daytime photos might struggle with nighttime photos, even of the same objects. The visual patterns are different enough that the AI's learned patterns don't transfer well.

Language Example: A language AI trained primarily on formal writing might struggle with heavy slang, dialect, or unconventional language use. The statistical patterns are too different from what it learned.

Conceptual Example: AI trained on contemporary data might struggle with questions about future scenarios or hypothetical situations that involve concepts or combinations it hasn't encountered in training.

Lack of True Generalization

Humans generalize remarkably well. If you learn about cars, you can reason about vehicles you've never seen, understand the concept of transportation generally, and apply relevant knowledge to boats, planes, or even hypothetical alien transport systems.

AI's generalization is much more limited. Each capability is specific to what was in the training data. It can't truly reason by analogy or apply concepts to fundamentally new domains the way humans can.

Why Generalization Is Hard: True generalization requires understanding underlying principles, not just surface patterns. You generalize from cars to boats because you understand the principle of vehicles as human-designed machines for transportation.

AI recognizes patterns but doesn't grasp underlying principles in this deeper sense. Its "generalization" is really interpolation within the pattern space it learned during training, not true conceptual generalization to entirely new domains.

Edge Cases and Adversarial Examples

AI is particularly vulnerable to edge cases—unusual situations at the boundaries of what it was trained on—and adversarial examples—inputs specifically designed to fool the AI.

Adversarial Images: Researchers have created images that look normal to humans but cause AI to misidentify them completely. By adding carefully crafted noise patterns invisible to humans, they can make an AI think a panda is a gibbon, or a stop sign is a speed limit sign.

This vulnerability exists because AI is doing pattern matching based on statistical features, not understanding what objects actually are. The adversarial noise shifts the statistical patterns in ways that fool the AI but don't change what humans perceive.

Adversarial Text: Similarly, carefully crafted text can confuse language AI. Small changes that don't affect human understanding can cause AI to produce very different outputs. This reveals that the AI isn't truly understanding meaning—it's sensitive to surface patterns in ways that true understanding wouldn't be.

Lack of Creativity

While AI can generate novel combinations and variations, its creativity is limited to recombining patterns from training data. It doesn't have genuine imagination or the ability to conceive of truly new concepts.

Human Creativity: Humans can imagine things that don't exist and have never existed. Science fiction writers imagine alien life forms fundamentally different from Earth life. Inventors create devices unlike anything before them. Artists develop entirely new art movements.

This creativity comes from understanding principles deeply enough to break and reconstruct them in new ways, from combining concepts in unprecedented manners, and from imagination grounded in but not limited by experience.

AI's Limitations: AI generates variations on patterns it learned. It can combine elements in new ways (a "cat riding a dragon" in an AI-generated image), but it's mixing learned patterns, not inventing fundamentally new concepts.

Ask an AI to invent a completely new color, or describe a sense humans don't have, or imagine mathematics with different axioms—tasks requiring conceptual creativity beyond recombination—and its limitations become apparent.

Limitation: No Real Learning From Interaction

Another crucial limitation: AI systems (in most current deployments) don't genuinely learn from their interactions with you.

The Training vs. Inference Distinction

Training Phase: AI learns during a training phase where it processes vast amounts of data and adjusts its parameters. This happens before you interact with it and requires enormous computational resources.

Inference Phase: When you use AI—asking questions, having conversations—the system is in "inference mode." It's applying its already-learned patterns to your input and generating outputs, but its core parameters aren't changing. It's not learning from you in any meaningful sense.

Why This Matters: This means if you correct an AI's mistake, it might acknowledge the correction in that conversation, but it won't remember it for next time. The correction doesn't actually teach it anything in a persistent way. Each conversation is largely independent, not part of an ongoing learning process.

Some systems now have "memory" features that store information about users, but this is different from genuine learning—it's more like taking notes than actually learning and integrating knowledge.

Contrast With Human Learning

Humans learn continuously from every interaction. If someone corrects you once, you typically remember. You integrate new information into your existing knowledge, adjusting your understanding.

AI's learning is locked in during training. After deployment, it's static (until retrained with new data, which is infrequent and computationally expensive). It can't adapt and improve through use the way humans naturally do.

This limitation means:

- AI makes the same mistakes repeatedly
- It can't adapt to your communication style over time (beyond what memory features provide)
- It doesn't become an expert in your specific needs through repeated interaction
- Teaching it something doesn't actually teach it in a persistent way

Limitation: No Consciousness or Self-Awareness

AI is not conscious. It has no inner experience, no self-awareness, no feelings, and no subjective experience of existence. This absence has important implications.

What Consciousness Involves

Consciousness includes:

- Subjective experience (what philosophers call "qualia")—what it's like to see red, feel pain, experience joy
- Self-awareness—knowing that you exist, have experiences, and are separate from others
- Intentionality—having thoughts *about* things, desires, goals, and purposes
- Unity of experience—integrating different sensory inputs into coherent experience

AI Has None of This

When an AI generates text, there's no "it" experiencing the process. There's no internal voice, no thoughts, no experience. The system processes inputs through mathematical operations and produces outputs, but there's no subjective experience accompanying this process.

Why This Matters:

No Genuine Understanding: Part of human understanding involves conscious experience. You don't just process the word "pain"—you know what pain feels like. This experiential knowledge is absent in AI.

No Genuine Emotions: When AI writes "I feel happy to help you," it's not actually feeling anything. It's generating text that fits patterns of helpful responses. The words are empty of actual feeling.

No Ethical Status: Without consciousness, AI has no interests, can't suffer, and can't be harmed in morally relevant ways. You can't be cruel to AI because there's nothing there to be cruel to. This is relevant for how we think about our obligations regarding AI.

No Authentic Relationship: When you have a conversation with AI, you're interacting with a pattern-generation system, not a conscious being. Any sense of relationship or connection is one-sided—you might feel it, but the AI doesn't.

The Hard Problem of Consciousness

We don't know if consciousness could ever arise in AI or if it requires biological substrates. This is called the "hard problem of consciousness"—explaining why and how subjective experience arises from physical processes.

Some philosophers think consciousness is computational and could potentially arise in sophisticated AI. Others think it requires biological processes, or is fundamentally non-physical, making artificial consciousness impossible.

What's certain is that current AI is not conscious, regardless of how conversational and sophisticated it seems.

Limitation: No Moral Judgment

Related to a lack of consciousness, AI lacks genuine moral understanding and cannot make authentic moral judgments.

Pattern Matching vs. Moral Understanding

AI can generate text that sounds morally sophisticated because it learned patterns in how humans discuss ethics. It can articulate principles like fairness, justice, and harm reduction.

But it doesn't truly understand these principles. It doesn't care about fairness, feel empathy for suffering, or value human dignity. It's matching patterns in ethical discourse, not making genuine moral judgments grounded in values.

The Alignment Problem

This creates the "AI alignment problem"—ensuring AI systems behave in ways aligned with human values even though the AI doesn't share or understand those values intrinsically.

We try to align AI through:

- Training on data that reflects human values
- Using human feedback to reward desired behaviors
- Implementing rules and constraints
- Testing for harmful outputs

But these are external constraints, not internal values. The AI isn't being ethical because it understands ethics—it's following patterns that correlate with ethical output.

Why This Limitation Matters

Cannot Handle Novel Moral Dilemmas: When facing moral situations not well-represented in training data, AI can't reason from genuine moral principles. It can only extrapolate patterns, which may fail in novel ethical territory.

No Moral Responsibility: AI cannot be held morally responsible for its outputs because it has no intentions, understanding, or agency. Responsibility for AI behavior falls on its creators and deployers, not the AI itself.

Risk of Harmful Advice: Because AI lacks moral understanding, it might generate harmful advice that sounds reasonable. It might suggest unethical actions without understanding why they're problematic if such patterns exist in training data.

Limitation: Brittle and Fragile

Despite impressive capabilities in many areas, AI is brittle—it works well within its domain but breaks easily when pushed outside it.

Narrow Success Conditions

AI systems typically perform well under conditions similar to those in the training data. Outside those conditions, they may fail dramatically.

An autonomous vehicle AI might drive excellently on clear, well-marked roads with typical traffic, but fail when encountering:

- Construction zones with unusual markings
- Extreme weather conditions
- Unusual obstacles not in training data
- Scenarios requiring creative problem-solving

The AI lacks robustness—it can't adapt flexibly to unexpected situations.

Small Changes, Big Effects

Sometimes, tiny changes that wouldn't affect human performance dramatically impact AI. Changing a single pixel in an image, rewording a question slightly, or altering context in subtle ways can cause completely different outputs.

This fragility reveals that AI isn't truly understanding—it's pattern matching in ways sensitive to features that wouldn't matter if genuine understanding were present.

No Graceful Degradation

Humans faced with situations they don't fully understand can often "muddle through" using general intelligence, common sense, and creativity. We degrade gracefully, performing worse but not completely failing.

AI often fails catastrophically when conditions deviate significantly from those in the training data. There's no graceful degradation because there's no underlying understanding to fall back on—just patterns that either apply or don't.

Living With AI's Limitations

Understanding AI's limitations is crucial for using it appropriately:

Verify AI Output

Never trust AI-generated information without verification, especially for important decisions. Always fact-check, especially for:

- Historical or factual claims
- Medical or legal advice
- Technical specifications
- News or current events
- Citations and references

Use AI as a Tool, Not an Authority

Treat AI as a sophisticated tool that can help with tasks, not as an authoritative source of truth or wisdom. It's useful for:

- Drafting initial content you'll edit
- Brainstorming ideas you'll evaluate
- Explaining concepts you'll verify
- Suggesting approaches you'll assess

Combine AI With Human Judgment

The best outcomes typically come from combining AI capabilities with human judgment, understanding, and common sense. Use AI to handle pattern-matching tasks where it excels, while providing the understanding, ethics, creativity, and common sense it lacks.

Recognize Context Limitations

Understand that AI works best within domains similar to its training data and may struggle with:

- Novel situations
- Specialized domains
- Cultural contexts underrepresented in training
- Cutting-edge developments after its training date
- Tasks requiring physical understanding

Monitor for Hallucinations

Be especially vigilant for confident-sounding but false information. If something seems questionable, verify it. If AI cites sources, check that they exist and say what the AI claims.

Provide Human Oversight

For important applications, maintain human oversight. Don't let AI make consequential decisions autonomously, especially in domains like healthcare, law, finance, or safety-critical systems where mistakes have serious consequences.

The Silver Lining: Human Intelligence Remains Special

Understanding AI's limitations isn't just about knowing what machines can't do—it also highlights what makes human intelligence special:

Genuine Understanding: Humans truly understand things through lived experience, not just pattern matching. This grounded understanding makes human knowledge qualitatively different from AI's statistical correlations.

Common Sense: The intuitive knowledge about how the world works that we acquire through living gives us robust intelligence that works across contexts. This common sense is remarkably difficult to replicate artificially.

True Learning: We continuously learn from every experience, integrating new knowledge into existing understanding. Our learning is lifelong, flexible, and doesn't require massive computational resources.

Consciousness and Values: Our subjective experience, self-awareness, and genuine values make us moral agents with intrinsic worth. These qualities aren't replicable in pattern-matching systems.

Creative Insight: Human creativity involves genuine imagination—the ability to conceive of fundamentally new concepts, not just recombine existing patterns.

Adaptability: Humans excel at novel situations, bringing creativity, intuition, and general intelligence to problems we've never encountered before.

Conclusion: Impressive But Fundamentally Limited

AI's recent capabilities are genuinely impressive. The ability to generate coherent text, create images, hold conversations, and assist with countless tasks represents real technological achievement.

But these capabilities coexist with fundamental limitations. AI doesn't truly understand, lacks common sense, makes mistakes with unwarranted confidence, struggles with novelty, and has no consciousness or genuine values.

These aren't bugs to be fixed in the next version—they're fundamental characteristics of how current AI works. The systems are doing sophisticated pattern matching and generation, not thinking, understanding, or experiencing.

This means:

- AI is a powerful tool, but needs human oversight
- AI output requires verification and can't be blindly trusted
- Tasks requiring understanding, judgment, creativity, or common sense still need humans
- The value of human intelligence, wisdom, and judgment hasn't diminished

Understanding these limitations helps us use AI appropriately—leveraging its strengths while compensating for its weaknesses with human capabilities. It also helps us appreciate what makes human intelligence special and irreplaceable.

As AI continues advancing, some limitations may be addressed. But fundamental differences between pattern recognition (however sophisticated) and true understanding suggest that certain limitations may persist. The question isn't whether AI can do impressive things—clearly it can—but whether pattern matching at scale can ever constitute genuine understanding.

For now, AI remains a powerful but limited tool, best used in combination with human intelligence, judgment, and understanding. Recognizing these limitations isn't pessimistic—it's realistic, helping us build appropriate expectations and use AI wisely while maintaining the human oversight, verification, and judgment that remain essential.

Nine
The Opportunities and Concerns of AI
Understanding Both Sides of the Revolution

AI can help doctors diagnose diseases, make work more efficient, and solve complex problems. But it also raises questions about job changes, privacy, bias in decision-making, and how we verify what's real versus AI-generated.

Artificial intelligence is neither purely beneficial nor purely harmful—it's a powerful technology with genuine opportunities to improve human life and serious concerns that require careful attention. Understanding both sides helps us maximize AI's benefits while mitigating its risks. Let's explore the opportunities AI presents and the concerns it raises, examining how this technology is reshaping society in complex ways.

OPPORTUNITIES: How AI Can Help Humanity

Healthcare: Saving Lives and Improving Diagnosis

One of AI's most promising applications is in healthcare, where it's already demonstrating life-saving potential.

Medical Image Analysis:

AI systems can analyze X-rays, MRIs, CT scans, and other medical images with remarkable accuracy. These systems have been trained on millions of medical images and can detect patterns that even experienced radiologists might miss.

For example, AI can identify early-stage lung cancer in chest X-rays, sometimes catching tumors so small that human doctors overlook them. Studies have shown that AI can match or exceed human radiologist performance in detecting certain conditions.

Why this matters: Early detection dramatically improves treatment success rates. If AI helps catch cancer or other diseases earlier, it directly saves lives. In healthcare systems facing radiologist shortages, AI can help process the backlog of images waiting for review.

Diagnostic Assistance:

AI systems can help doctors diagnose diseases by analyzing patient symptoms, medical history, test results, and comparing them to vast databases of medical knowledge. IBM's Watson Health and similar systems can suggest possible diagnoses and relevant research that physicians might not have considered.

These systems don't replace doctor judgment but augment it—providing a "second opinion" that considers more data and medical literature than any human could retain. They're particularly valuable for rare diseases where individual doctors might see only a few cases in their careers.

Drug Discovery:

Traditionally, developing new drugs takes 10-15 years and costs billions of dollars. Much of this time involves testing millions of potential molecular compounds to find ones that might be effective.

AI can dramatically accelerate this process by predicting which molecular structures are likely to be effective against specific diseases, narrowing the search space from millions of possibilities to thousands of promising candidates. This doesn't eliminate testing but makes it far more efficient.

During the COVID-19 pandemic, AI helped identify existing drugs that might be repurposed for treatment and accelerated vaccine development by predicting protein structures and interactions.

Personalized Medicine:

AI can analyze individual patient characteristics—genetic profile, medical history, lifestyle factors—to recommend personalized treatment plans. What works for one patient might not work for another with the same disease, and AI can help identify which treatments are most likely to be effective for each specific person.

This personalization can improve outcomes and reduce side effects by avoiding treatments unlikely to work for particular individuals.

Remote Monitoring:

AI-powered wearable devices and smartphone apps can continuously monitor health indicators—heart rate, activity levels, sleep patterns, blood glucose—and alert patients and doctors to concerning changes before they become emergencies.

For chronic conditions like diabetes or heart disease, this continuous monitoring can prevent complications and help patients manage their conditions more effectively.

The Healthcare Opportunity Summary:

AI in healthcare represents an opportunity to:

- Catch diseases earlier when they're more treatable
- Reduce diagnostic errors
- Make expert-level analysis available in underserved areas
- Accelerate medical research and drug development
- Personalize treatment to individual patients
- Monitor health continuously rather than just during doctor visits

These capabilities could extend lives, improve quality of life, and make healthcare more accessible and effective.

Work Efficiency: Doing More With Less Effort

AI can handle routine, repetitive tasks, freeing humans to focus on work requiring creativity, judgment, and human connection.

Automating Tedious Tasks:

Consider tasks that consume enormous time but don't require much creativity:

- Data entry and organization
- Scheduling meetings by finding times that work for everyone
- Sorting and prioritizing emails
- Generating routine reports
- Transcribing meetings and interviews
- Creating first drafts of standard documents

AI can handle these tasks faster and more accurately than humans, reclaiming time for more valuable work. A marketing professional might spend 20% of their time on administrative tasks and 80% on creative strategy—AI could flip this ratio, handling the administrative work so they focus on strategy.

Enhancing Human Capabilities:

Rather than replacing workers, AI often enhances their capabilities:

A writer using AI can:

- Generate outlines to overcome writer's block
- Get suggestions for improving clarity
- Check grammar and style instantly
- Research topics more efficiently

A designer using AI can:

- Generate multiple design variations quickly
- Remove backgrounds from images automatically
- Create initial mockups to refine
- Test different color schemes rapidly

A programmer using AI can:

- Write boilerplate code automatically
- Debug problems faster
- Get suggestions for better approaches
- Document code automatically

In each case, the human remains in control, making creative decisions and exercising judgment, while AI handles routine aspects of the work.

Accelerating Research:

Scientists and researchers use AI to:

- Analyze vast datasets too large for manual analysis
- Identify patterns in experimental data
- Search through millions of research papers to find relevant studies
- Generate hypotheses to test
- Simulate complex systems

This acceleration can speed up scientific discovery across fields from climate science to materials engineering to social science.

Improving Customer Service:

AI chatbots handle routine customer service inquiries 24/7, providing instant responses to common questions. This frees human customer service representatives to handle complex issues requiring empathy, judgment, and creative problem-solving.

The result: customers get faster service for simple issues, and human representatives handle more interesting, meaningful work rather than answering the same basic questions repeatedly.

The Efficiency Opportunity Summary:

AI's ability to handle routine tasks creates opportunities to:

- Reduce time spent on tedious work
- Focus human effort on creative and strategic work
- Accomplish more with the same resources
- Make expertise more accessible and scalable
- Accelerate research and innovation
- Improve response times and availability

This efficiency doesn't necessarily mean fewer jobs—it means different jobs, potentially more fulfilling ones focused on uniquely human capabilities.

Solving Complex Problems

Some problems are so complex that human analysis alone struggles to solve them. AI can help tackle these challenges.

Climate and Environmental Science:

Climate systems involve countless interacting variables—ocean temperatures, atmospheric conditions, solar radiation, vegetation patterns, and more. AI can:

- Process climate data from thousands of sensors worldwide
- Model climate systems with unprecedented detail
- Predict extreme weather events earlier and more accurately
- Optimize renewable energy systems
- Identify efficient carbon capture strategies

These capabilities help us better understand and respond to climate change.

Traffic and Urban Planning:

AI can optimize traffic flow in cities by:

- Adjusting traffic light timing based on real-time traffic
- Predicting congestion and suggesting alternative routes
- Planning public transportation schedules based on actual usage patterns
- Simulating the impact of infrastructure changes before building them

Cities using AI for traffic management have reduced congestion, shortened commute times, and reduced emissions from idling vehicles.

Energy Grid Optimization:

Electrical grids must balance supply and demand second by second. AI can:

- Predict energy demand patterns
- Optimize when to use different energy sources
- Integrate variable renewable energy (solar, wind) more effectively
- Identify grid problems before they cause outages
- Reduce energy waste

This makes energy systems more efficient, reliable, and sustainable.

Agricultural Optimization:

AI helps farmers:

- Monitor crop health using satellite and drone imagery
- Predict optimal planting and harvesting times

- Apply water and fertilizer precisely where needed rather than uniformly
- Detect pest infestations early
- Predict yields

Precision agriculture using AI can increase food production while reducing water usage, chemical runoff, and environmental impact.

Scientific Discovery:

AI has contributed to breakthroughs across sciences:

- Predicting protein structures (AlphaFold), accelerating biological research
- Discovering new materials with desired properties
- Identifying potential asteroids that could threaten Earth
- Analyzing particle physics data to discover new particles
- Finding patterns in genetic data linked to diseases

These discoveries advance human knowledge and solve problems that seemed intractable.

The Complex Problem-Solving Opportunity Summary:

AI's ability to process vast data and identify subtle patterns creates opportunities to:

- Address climate change more effectively
- Improve infrastructure and urban systems
- Advance scientific understanding
- Increase food production sustainably
- Optimize energy systems
- Tackle problems too complex for human analysis alone

These applications have the potential to improve the quality of life globally and address existential challenges facing humanity.

Accessibility and Democratization

AI can make capabilities once available only to experts accessible to everyone.

Language Translation:

Real-time translation AI breaks down language barriers, enabling:

- Communication between people who speak different languages
- Access to information in any language
- International business and collaboration
- Travelers navigating foreign countries independently

This democratizes communication, making the world more connected.

Education:

AI tutoring systems can:

- Provide personalized instruction adapted to each student's pace
- Offer education in areas lacking qualified teachers
- Make learning accessible 24/7 without expensive tutors
- Explain concepts in multiple ways until students understand
- Provide practice problems at appropriate difficulty levels

This makes quality education more accessible regardless of location or economic circumstances.

Professional Tools:

AI puts professional-grade tools in everyone's hands:

- Photo and video editing that once required expert skills
- Graphic design capabilities
- Writing assistance and editing
- Music composition tools

- Legal document generation for common needs

Skills that once required years of training or expensive professional services have become accessible to anyone.

Assistive Technology:

AI helps people with disabilities:

- Screen readers that describe images to visually impaired users
- Real-time captioning for deaf and hard-of-hearing individuals
- Predictive text that helps people with motor difficulties type faster
- Voice control for those who can't use traditional interfaces
- AI that can detect falls or medical emergencies and call for help

These technologies increase independence and quality of life.

CONCERNS: What We Need to Worry About

While opportunities are significant, AI also raises legitimate concerns that require attention.

Job Displacement and Economic Disruption

Perhaps the most widespread concern is AI's impact on employment.

Which Jobs Are at Risk:

AI threatens jobs involving routine, predictable tasks:

- Data entry and processing
- Basic bookkeeping and accounting
- Customer service for simple inquiries
- Routine legal document preparation
- Basic writing and content generation
- Driving (as autonomous vehicles develop)

- Manufacturing and warehouse work
- Some aspects of radiology and pathology
- Translation and transcription

Studies suggest that 30-40% of current job tasks could be automated by AI, though complete job elimination is less common—usually, AI automates part of a job, not the entire job.

The Historical Pattern:

Technology has always disrupted employment. The Industrial Revolution eliminated many agricultural and craft jobs while creating factory jobs. Computers eliminated typing pools and many clerical positions while creating IT jobs.

The pattern: technology destroys some jobs while creating others, but the transition is painful for displaced workers, and new jobs may require different skills than old ones.

Why This Time Might Be Different:

Some economists argue AI could be different because:

- It affects cognitive work, not just physical labor
- The pace of change is faster than previous disruptions
- AI could eventually handle many tasks currently requiring human intelligence
- New jobs might also be automatable by AI

Others argue we'll adapt as always, finding new, valuable work for humans as AI handles routine tasks.

The Real Concern:

Even if the total number of jobs doesn't decrease, the transition is painful. A 50-year-old truck driver displaced by autonomous vehicles can't easily retrain as a data scientist. Communities built around specific industries face disruption when AI changes those industries.

The concern isn't just about unemployment numbers—it's about human dignity, community stability, and whether the economic benefits of AI are shared broadly or concentrated among AI owners.

Potential Responses:

Addressing this concern requires:

- Retraining programs to help workers adapt
- Education systems that prepare students for an AI world
- Social safety nets for displaced workers
- Policies that distribute AI benefits broadly
- Focus on jobs emphasizing uniquely human skills (creativity, empathy, judgment)

Privacy and Surveillance

AI's capabilities enable unprecedented surveillance and data collection, raising serious privacy concerns.

How AI Threatens Privacy:

Facial Recognition Everywhere: AI can identify individuals in photos and videos instantly. Governments and companies could track people's movements through networks of cameras, knowing where you go, who you meet, and what you do.

China's social credit system uses this technology extensively. Cities worldwide are deploying facial recognition, often without clear rules about how data is used or stored.

Behavioral Tracking: AI analyzes your online behavior—what you click, how long you read articles, what you purchase, who you communicate with—building detailed profiles of your interests, beliefs, and habits.

These profiles can be used for targeted advertising but also for manipulation, discrimination, or control.

Data Aggregation: AI can combine data from multiple sources—your social media, purchase history, location data, browsing history, health information—to infer things you never explicitly shared, like political views, sexual orientation, health conditions, or financial status.

Inference From Public Data: Even if you're privacy-conscious, AI can infer information about you from public data: your friends' social media posts (which might tag you or mention you), public records, professional profiles, and more.

Voice and Communication Analysis: AI can analyze voice calls to detect emotion, stress, or deception. It can scan emails and messages for keywords. This enables surveillance at a scale previously impossible.

The Chilling Effect:

When people know they're constantly monitored and analyzed, it changes behavior. They might avoid certain searches, conversations, or associations, fearing judgment or consequences. This self-censorship undermines freedom even if no explicit restrictions exist.

Who Has This Power:

Privacy concerns involve both governments and private companies. Governments might use AI for social control. Companies might use it for profit, potentially selling access to your data or using it in ways you didn't anticipate when you agreed to the terms of service.

The Privacy Concern Summary:

AI enables surveillance and data analysis at unprecedented scale, threatening:

- Personal privacy and autonomy
- Freedom from constant monitoring
- Control over your own information
- Protection from manipulation based on detailed personal profiles

Addressing this requires strong privacy regulations, transparency about data collection, and limits on AI surveillance capabilities.

Bias and Fairness in Decision-Making

AI systems can perpetuate or amplify human biases, leading to unfair outcomes.

How Bias Enters AI Systems:

Training Data Reflects Historical Bias: AI learns from data generated by humans, which reflects human biases. Historical lending data might show that banks approved fewer loans for certain demographic groups—not because those groups were less creditworthy, but due to discrimination. An AI trained on this data learns the discriminatory patterns.

Measurement Bias: If arrest records are used to train crime prediction AI and certain neighborhoods are policed more heavily, the data will show higher crime rates in those areas, even if actual crime rates are similar elsewhere. The AI learns to target already over-policed areas, perpetuating the problem.

Representation Bias: If training data doesn't include diverse examples, AI performs poorly on underrepresented groups. Facial recognition trained mostly on white faces performs worse on people of color. Speech recognition trained on standard American accents struggles with other accents.

Designer Bias: The people designing AI systems—disproportionately male, white, and from wealthy countries—might not recognize how their systems affect different communities, inadvertently building in biases.

Real-World Examples:

Hiring AI: Amazon developed an AI recruiting tool that downgraded resumes containing the word "women's" (as in "women's chess club") because it learned from historical hiring data in which men were hired more often for technical roles. The system learned to prefer male candidates.

Criminal Justice: Risk assessment tools used in sentencing and parole decisions have been shown to incorrectly label Black defendants as higher risk than white defendants with similar backgrounds, likely due to biased historical data.

Lending: AI systems that determine creditworthiness have sometimes denied loans to qualified applicants from minority communities at higher rates, potentially due to learning from historically discriminatory lending patterns.

Healthcare: An AI used to identify patients needing additional medical care systematically referred fewer Black patients than equally sick white patients because it used healthcare spending as a proxy for health needs, but Black patients historically received less care and thus had lower spending, even when equally sick.

Why Bias Is Particularly Concerning in AI:

- **Scale:** Biased human decisions affect individuals; biased AI affects millions
- **Opacity:** It's often unclear why AI made a particular decision, making bias hard to detect
- **Authority:** AI decisions are often treated as objective and unquestionable
- **Automation:** Biased outcomes happen without human review or accountability
- **Persistence:** Once bias is embedded in a deployed system, it continues affecting people until the system is fixed

The Fairness Concern Summary:

AI can encode and scale human biases, leading to:

- Discriminatory outcomes in hiring, lending, criminal justice, and healthcare
- Perpetuation of historical inequities
- Harm to already marginalized communities
- Decisions that seem objective but are actually biased

Addressing this requires:

- Diverse teams building AI
- Careful auditing for bias
- Diverse, representative training data
- Transparency about how AI makes decisions
- Accountability when AI causes harm

Misinformation and Truth Verification

AI's ability to generate realistic content threatens our ability to distinguish truth from falsehood.

The Deepfake Problem:

AI can create:

- **Fake videos** of people saying things they never said ("deepfakes")
- **Fake audio** in someone's voice saying anything
- **Fake images** of events that never happened
- **Fake documents** that look authentic

As this technology improves, distinguishing real from fake becomes increasingly difficult.

Political and Social Consequences:

Election Interference: Imagine a fake video of a political candidate saying something offensive released days before an election. Even if quickly debunked, millions might see it and believe it, potentially swaying the election.

Undermining Trust: When anyone can fake anything, people might stop believing real evidence. A politician could dismiss genuine scandalous recordings as "deepfakes," and followers might believe them. Truth becomes whatever people want to believe.

Personal Attacks: Malicious actors could create fake compromising images or videos of anyone—politicians, activists, ordinary people—to harass, blackmail, or destroy reputations.

Historical Revision: Fake historical images or documents could muddy our understanding of the past, making history seem uncertain and contested.

Synthetic Content Flooding:

AI can generate content so rapidly that it could flood social media, comment sections, and online forums with:

- Fake product reviews
- Fake news articles
- Fake social media accounts posting propaganda
- Fake grassroots movements (actually AI-generated)

This "information pollution" makes it difficult to find genuine information.

Sophisticated Scams:

AI enables more convincing scams:

- Emails that perfectly mimic someone's writing style
- Voice calls that sound exactly like a relative claiming they need emergency money
- Fake websites and documents that appear completely legitimate

- Personalized phishing attacks based on AI analysis of your social media

Journalism Challenges:

Journalists face increased difficulty verifying information when:

- Images and videos can be completely fabricated
- Documents can be forged perfectly
- Sources might be AI-generated fakes
- Claims can be supported by fake but convincing evidence

The Verification Concern Summary:

AI-generated content threatens:

- Our ability to verify truth
- Trust in media and evidence
- Democratic processes
- Personal reputation and safety
- Shared understanding of reality

Addressing this requires:

- Technology to detect AI-generated content
- Digital signatures and authentication systems
- Media literacy education
- Platforms taking responsibility for synthetic content
- Legal consequences for malicious fake content creation

Concentration of Power

AI might concentrate power in fewer hands, raising concerns about corporate and governmental control.

Who Controls AI:

Developing cutting-edge AI requires:

- Enormous computing resources (millions of dollars in hardware)
- Vast amounts of data
- Specialized expertise
- Significant financial resources for research and development

Only large tech companies and well-funded organizations can afford this, creating a concentration of AI capability among a few entities: Google, Microsoft, Meta, OpenAI, Amazon, and a few others, plus government organizations.

The Power Imbalance:

These organizations control AI systems that millions of people rely on, yet users have little say in how they operate. The companies decide:

- What data to train on
- What values to embed in the system
- What the AI will and won't do
- Who gets access and on what terms
- How the AI shapes the information people see

This gives enormous power to a small number of tech executives.

Economic Concentration:

AI might accelerate wealth concentration. Companies with the best AI can:

- Operate more efficiently than competitors
- Provide better services
- Attract more customers and data
- Improve their AI further with that data

This creates a virtuous cycle for winners and a vicious cycle for losers, potentially leading to "winner-take-all" markets where one or two AI-powered companies dominate each industry.

Governmental Power:

Governments with advanced AI capabilities have unprecedented power:

- Surveillance and social control
- Military advantages
- Economic planning and control
- Information management and propaganda

This could enable authoritarianism at scales previously impossible, or give certain nations overwhelming advantages over others.

The Control Concern Summary:

AI could concentrate power by:

- Placing capabilities in the hands of few organizations
- Enabling unprecedented surveillance and control
- Creating winner-take-all economics
- Giving enormous influence to those who control AI

Addressing this requires:

- Open-source AI to democratize access
- Regulation preventing abuse of AI power
- Antitrust enforcement preventing monopolies
- International cooperation on AI governance
- Public participation in decisions about AI development

Security and Weaponization

AI creates new security challenges and could make weapons more dangerous.

Cybersecurity Threats:

AI can:

- Find vulnerabilities in software faster than humans
- Generate sophisticated phishing attacks personalized to targets
- Automate hacking attempts at scale
- Evade security systems by learning their patterns

This makes cyberattacks more frequent and sophisticated, threatening critical infrastructure, financial systems, and personal data.

Autonomous Weapons:

AI-powered weapons that select and engage targets without human control raise concerns:

- Removing humans from life-or-death decisions
- Lowering barriers to violence (no soldiers at risk)
- Unpredictable behavior in complex situations
- Arms races in autonomous weapons
- Non-state actors accessing advanced weapons

Many AI researchers advocate for bans on autonomous weapons, but development continues.

Misinformation Campaigns:

Hostile nations could use AI to:

- Generate propaganda at a massive scale

- Create fake social media accounts to spread division
- Produce deepfakes of leaders during crises
- Manipulate public opinion systematically

Biological Threats:

AI could assist in designing biological weapons or predicting how to engineer dangerous pathogens. While AI also helps defend against these threats, the dual-use nature is concerning.

The Security Concern Summary:

AI creates security challenges through:

- Enhanced cyberattack capabilities
- Autonomous weapons
- Sophisticated information warfare
- Potential for biological threats
- Lowered barriers to sophisticated attacks

Addressing this requires:

- International agreements limiting dangerous applications
- Robust AI security research
- Responsible disclosure of AI capabilities
- Controls on dual-use AI research

Balancing Opportunities and Concerns

The question isn't whether AI has opportunities or concerns—it clearly has both. The challenge is maximizing benefits while minimizing harms.

Principles for Beneficial AI

Human Oversight: Keep humans in the loop for important decisions. AI should assist and augment human judgment, not replace it entirely, especially in high-stakes situations.

Transparency: People affected by AI decisions should understand how those decisions were made. "The AI said so" isn't acceptable for consequential decisions about healthcare, employment, or justice.

Accountability: When AI causes harm, someone—the developers, deployers, or users—must be accountable. We need legal frameworks establishing responsibility.

Fairness: AI systems should be regularly audited for bias and fairness. Systems showing discriminatory patterns should be fixed or discontinued.

Privacy Protection: Strict limits on data collection and use, with meaningful consent and the ability to opt out of AI analysis.

Security: AI systems must be secured against misuse, and dangerous applications should be restricted.

Inclusive Development: AI development should include diverse voices —different genders, races, cultures, and perspectives—to catch problems that homogeneous teams might miss.

Benefit Sharing: AI's economic benefits should be broadly distributed rather than concentrated among a few. This might require new policies, regulations, or economic structures.

The Role of Regulation

Appropriate regulation can maximize benefits while minimizing harms:

What to Regulate:

- High-risk applications (criminal justice, healthcare, hiring) requiring human oversight and fairness audits
- Privacy protections limiting data collection and use
- Transparency requirements for AI decision-making
- Restrictions on surveillance technology
- Rules against malicious deepfakes and misinformation
- Safety standards for autonomous systems
- Antitrust enforcement preventing monopolies

What Not to Over-Regulate:

- Beneficial research and development
- Applications with low risk of harm
- Open-source AI development that democratizes access
- Innovation that creates opportunities

The goal is smart regulation that prevents harm without stifling beneficial innovation.

Individual Responsibility

Individuals also have roles in ensuring AI benefits society:

- **Stay Informed:** Understand AI capabilities and limitations. Be aware of when you're interacting with AI.
- **Verify Information:** Don't trust AI-generated content without verification. Be skeptical of information online.
- **Protect Privacy:** Be thoughtful about the data you share. Use privacy tools when appropriate.
- **Demand Accountability:** Support regulations and policies that hold AI developers accountable. Choose products and services from responsible companies.

- **Provide Feedback:** When AI systems behave inappropriately, report it. Companies often rely on user reports to identify problems.
- **Use Thoughtfully:** Use AI tools for beneficial purposes, not harmful ones. Consider the implications of your use.

Conclusion: Navigating the AI Era

AI presents genuine opportunities to improve healthcare, increase productivity, solve complex problems, and make capabilities more accessible. These benefits are real and significant.

But AI also raises legitimate concerns about job displacement, privacy, bias, misinformation, concentrated power, and security. These risks are also real and require serious attention.

The future isn't predetermined. Whether AI becomes primarily beneficial or harmful depends on the choices we make:

- How we develop and deploy AI systems
- What regulations do we enact
- How we distribute benefits and manage disruptions
- Whether we prioritize human welfare over profit
- How we balance innovation with safety

Understanding both opportunities and concerns enables informed participation in these crucial decisions. Rather than uncritical enthusiasm or reflexive fear, we need thoughtful engagement with AI's complexities.

The goal should be shaping AI development to:

- Maximize benefits for humanity broadly
- Minimize harms and risks
- Ensure fairness and accountability
- Preserve human agency and dignity

- Address rather than exacerbate inequality
- Protect privacy and truth
- Maintain human values and judgment

This requires cooperation among technologists, policymakers, civil society, and the public. The stakes are high—AI will shape the future of work, healthcare, information, privacy, and power structures. Getting it right matters enormously.

The AI era has arrived. The question now is: what kind of AI future will we create? One that serves humanity's best interests, or one that creates new problems while solving old ones? The answer depends on recognizing both opportunities and concerns, then acting thoughtfully to maximize the former while mitigating the latter.

This is the challenge and responsibility of our time.

Ten
You're Part of the Conversation
Why Your Voice Matters in Shaping AI's Future

As AI becomes more common, we're all figuring out together how to use it responsibly, what rules make sense, and how to make sure it benefits everyone. Your perspective on how it should work in society actually matters.

When people think about artificial intelligence development, they often imagine it happening in distant research labs, controlled by tech giants and elite scientists. They assume decisions about AI are made by experts far removed from everyday life, and that ordinary people have no say in how this powerful technology evolves. This assumption is wrong—and dangerously so. The truth is that everyone affected by AI, which increasingly means everyone, has a legitimate role in shaping how AI develops and how society uses it. Your perspective matters, your concerns are valid, and your participation in the conversation about AI is both welcome and necessary.

Why This Isn't Just a Technical Issue

The first crucial point to understand is that AI isn't merely a technical challenge for engineers to solve. It's a social, ethical, political, and human challenge that affects everyone.

AI Touches Every Aspect of Life

AI already influences:

- Whether you get hired for a job
- What interest rate you're offered on a loan
- What information you see on social media
- How police patrol your neighborhood
- What medical treatments doctors recommend
- What educational opportunities you're offered
- Who you're matched with on dating apps
- What price you're charged for products
- Whether you're approved for housing
- How courts assess criminal defendants

These aren't technical questions—they're questions about fairness, justice, opportunity, and human dignity. The people affected by these AI systems have essential perspectives on whether they're working properly and fairly.

Technical Expertise Isn't Enough

Engineers can build AI systems that work technically—that process data, make predictions, and generate outputs. But engineers alone cannot determine:

- **What problems AI should solve:** Should we prioritize AI for healthcare, military applications, advertising, entertainment, or climate solutions? These are value judgments about societal priorities.
- **What trade-offs are acceptable:** If AI improves efficiency but costs jobs, is that acceptable? If it improves security but reduces privacy, where's the right balance? These aren't technical questions—they're ethical and political ones.
- **What outcomes are fair:** Is it fair if an AI system is highly accurate overall but performs poorly for a minority group? Engineers can measure accuracy, but "fairness" is a social determination that varies across cultures and contexts.

- **What risks are tolerable:** How much risk of AI making mistakes in medical diagnosis is acceptable? How autonomous should weapons systems be? These are societal choices, not purely technical ones.
- **What AI should never do:** Should AI be used for mass surveillance? Should it make parole decisions? Should it manipulate people's emotions for profit? These ethical boundaries must be set by society, not just technologists.

Engineers build what society asks them to build and operate within the rules society creates. If society doesn't participate in that conversation, engineers will build according to their own values and assumptions, which may not represent everyone's interests.

History Shows the Danger of Leaving It to Experts

History offers cautionary examples of technologies developed primarily by experts without sufficient public input:

Nuclear weapons were developed by physicists who later regretted the lack of broader societal discussion about whether to build them and how to control them. Some Manhattan Project scientists spent their later lives advocating for arms control, wishing society had been more involved in decisions about nuclear technology.

Social media platforms were built by technologists optimizing for "engagement" without sufficient consideration of impacts on mental health, democracy, or social cohesion. Only after societal harms became apparent did broader conversations about regulation and responsibility begin.

Genetic engineering proceeded rapidly in research labs until public concern led to the Asilomar Conference, where scientists agreed to self-imposed restrictions and called for public involvement in decisions about genetic modification.

In each case, limiting the conversation to experts led to problems that broader societal input might have prevented or mitigated. AI is potentially more consequential than any of these technologies, making public participation even more critical.

What "Being Part of the Conversation" Actually Means

When we say you're part of the conversation about AI, what does that actually look like? How do ordinary people participate in shaping AI's development and use?

Sharing Your Experiences and Concerns

One of the most valuable contributions anyone can make is simply reporting their experiences with AI systems and expressing concerns about how they're being used.

Personal Experience Matters:

If you've experienced an AI system behaving unfairly, that information is valuable:

- A resume screening AI that seems to discriminate
- A social media algorithm that amplifies harmful content
- A customer service chatbot that fails to help
- A recommendation system that creates filter bubbles
- A pricing algorithm that charges different prices to different people

Reporting these experiences helps identify problems that developers might not see from their perspective. Tech companies often don't know their systems are failing until users tell them. Researchers studying AI fairness rely on real-world reports of discriminatory outcomes.

Your experience isn't just an anecdote—it's data about how AI actually works in the real world, which is different from how it works in controlled tests. Problems that affect you likely affect many others, and speaking up helps bring those problems to light.

Your Concerns Aren't Dismissed:

When you're worried about AI—whether it's about job displacement, privacy, misinformation, or something else—that concern is legitimate and worth expressing. You don't need technical expertise to identify that something feels wrong or worry about AI's impact on your life.

Historically, public concerns about technology have often preceded expert recognition of problems. Parents raised concerns about social media's impact on teen mental health long before researchers confirmed those effects. Privacy advocates warned about surveillance risks before data breaches made headlines.

Your concerns help set the agenda for what researchers study, what policymakers address, and what companies prioritize. When enough people express concern about an issue, it becomes impossible to ignore.

Participating in Public Discussions

AI governance increasingly involves public consultation—opportunities for anyone to participate in shaping rules and norms.

Public Comment Periods:

Government agencies developing AI regulations typically have public comment periods during which anyone can submit input. In the United States, the Federal Trade Commission, Federal Communications Commission, and other agencies solicit public comments on AI-related rules.

These aren't just for experts. Comments from ordinary people affected by AI carry weight. A teacher's perspective on AI in education, a patient's perspective on AI in healthcare, or a worker's perspective on AI in hiring all provide essential context that regulators need.

Most people don't participate in these processes, which means the comments come disproportionately from tech companies and advocacy groups. Broader participation would create more balanced input.

Town Halls and Public Forums:

Many cities, universities, and organizations host public discussions about AI. These forums provide opportunities to:

- Learn about AI developments
- Ask questions of experts
- Share perspectives and concerns
- Discuss local AI issues
- Influence community decisions about AI use

Attending and participating in these forums makes you part of the conversation in a direct, tangible way.

Online Discussions:

Social media, comment sections, forums, and online communities provide spaces to discuss AI. While these can be chaotic, they also shape public opinion and sometimes directly influence decision-makers who monitor public sentiment.

Thoughtful participation in online discussions—sharing information, asking questions, raising concerns, challenging assumptions—contributes to the broader conversation about AI.

Voting and Political Engagement

AI is increasingly a political issue, and political engagement is a powerful way to shape AI's role in society.

AI as a Political Issue:

Politicians are beginning to propose AI policies:

- Regulations on AI use in hiring, lending, and criminal justice
- Privacy protections limiting AI surveillance
- Requirements for transparency in AI decision-making
- Restrictions on specific AI applications
- Funding for AI research and development
- Education and retraining programs for workers affected by AI

How politicians approach these issues depends partly on what constituents communicate as priorities. If voters make clear they care about AI issues, politicians respond.

Contacting Representatives:

Contacting elected officials—through calls, emails, letters, or meetings—about AI concerns is direct participation in democratic governance. When representatives hear repeatedly about an issue from constituents, it rises on their priority list.

You don't need to propose specific policy solutions. Simply communicating concerns and priorities helps: "I'm worried about AI surveillance in our community," "I'm concerned about AI replacing jobs without support for workers," "I want stronger privacy protections against AI data collection."

Voting Based on AI Positions:

As AI becomes more politically salient, politicians' positions on AI issues can become voting considerations. Supporting candidates with thoughtful, responsible approaches to AI governance helps shape policy.

Local Politics:

AI governance isn't just national. Local decisions matter too:

- Should your city use facial recognition in public spaces?
- Should your school district allow AI writing tools?
- Should your local police use predictive policing algorithms?
- Should municipal services use AI for decisions about residents?

These local issues often allow for more direct participation through city council meetings, school board meetings, and community forums.

Consumer Choices and Market Influence

How you choose to use (or not use) AI products and services influences how companies develop and deploy AI.

Choosing Responsible Companies:

Companies compete for customers, and customer preferences influence corporate behavior. If consumers prefer companies that:

- Use AI responsibly and transparently
- Protect user privacy
- Avoid manipulative AI practices
- Test for and mitigate AI bias
- Employ workers fairly despite AI automation

Then, companies have incentives to behave accordingly. Consumer choices won't solve all problems, but they create market pressure for responsible AI development.

Providing Feedback:

Companies want to know what users think. Providing feedback about AI features—what works, what doesn't, what concerns you—influences product development. Companies track user satisfaction, feature usage, and complaints, adjusting products based on this information.

When many users complain about an AI feature, companies often change it. When users praise something, companies invest more in it. Your individual feedback might seem small, but aggregated across many users, it shapes corporate decisions.

Terms of Service and Consent:

While terms of service are often impractical to read, making informed choices about what you agree to matters. If enough people decline services with invasive AI practices, companies notice.

Increasingly, privacy regulations like GDPR (in Europe) and CCPA (in California) give users rights to know how their data is used and to opt out. Exercising these rights signals that privacy matters to users, encouraging more protective practices.

Workplace Advocacy

For many people, AI's most direct impact is at work. Workplace advocacy shapes how employers deploy AI.

Asking Questions:

When employers introduce AI systems, workers can and should ask:

- How will this AI affect my job?
- What decisions will AI make, and what oversight exists?
- How was the AI trained, and has it been tested for bias?
- What happens if the AI makes mistakes?
- How will performance be evaluated—by AI metrics or human judgment?
- What retraining or support is available as AI changes job requirements?

These questions push employers to think carefully about AI deployment and treat workers fairly in the process.

Collective Bargaining:

In unionized workplaces, AI deployment can be subject to collective bargaining. Unions can negotiate:

- Limits on how AI is used for surveillance or evaluation

- Requirements for human oversight of AI decisions
- Protections against AI-driven job elimination
- Retraining opportunities
- Transparency about AI systems

Even in non-unionized workplaces, workers organizing to express concerns about AI creates pressure for responsible deployment.

Professional Standards:

Professional associations in many fields are developing guidelines for AI use. Participating in these associations and conversations helps shape professional standards that influence how AI is used in your field.

Education and Awareness

Becoming informed about AI and helping others understand it is itself a form of participation in the conversation.

Learning About AI:

Understanding AI basics—what it can and can't do, how it works, what risks it poses—enables more informed participation in discussions and decisions. You don't need to become an expert, but basic literacy helps.

Resources are increasingly available: online courses, articles, videos, books, and community education programs. As you learn, you become better equipped to contribute to conversations about AI.

Teaching Others:

Sharing what you learn with family, friends, colleagues, and community members multiplies your impact. AI literacy is low in the general population, and peer education is powerful.

Explaining to a parent how social media algorithms work, discussing with coworkers how AI might affect your industry, or helping friends understand AI privacy issues spreads awareness and enables broader participation in the conversation.

Media Literacy:

Understanding how to critically evaluate information about AI—distinguishing hype from reality, recognizing fearmongering versus legitimate concerns, and identifying who benefits from particular narratives—helps you participate more effectively in discussions.

Why Your Perspective Specifically Matters

You might think, "I'm not an expert, so why would my perspective matter?" There are several reasons why non-expert perspectives are not just valuable but essential.

You Represent Real-World Use and Impact

AI developers work in specific contexts—often well-resourced tech companies in wealthy areas. They may not understand how AI affects:

- People in different economic circumstances
- Different cultural communities
- People with disabilities
- Older adults less familiar with technology
- Rural communities with different needs than urban ones
- Workers in industries facing automation
- Students in under-resourced schools

Your lived experience provides essential context that developers lack. If you're a teacher, you understand classroom realities that AI education tool developers might miss. If you're a small business owner, you understand needs different from large corporations. If you're elderly, you experience technology accessibility issues that younger developers might not consider.

These perspectives aren't less valuable than technical expertise—they're different and complementary. Good AI development requires both technical skill and understanding of real-world context.

You Have Ethical and Value Perspectives

Technical experts can build AI to optimize for any goal, but which goals to pursue involves value judgments where everyone's input is relevant.

Different Communities Have Different Values:

What's considered "fair" varies across cultures and communities. Individualistic cultures might prioritize individual opportunity, while collectivist cultures might prioritize group harmony. Different religious traditions have different ethical frameworks. Different political philosophies lead to different views on acceptable trade-offs.

There's no objectively "correct" value system. In diverse democratic societies, AI should reflect broadly shared values arrived at through inclusive conversation, not just the values of developers.

You're Affected, So You Should Have a Say:

A basic democratic principle: those affected by decisions should participate in making them. If AI affects your job, your neighborhood, your healthcare, your children's education—you have legitimate standing to participate in decisions about how it's used.

This isn't just philosophical. Research shows that technologies developed without input from affected communities often fail or cause unintended harm. Participatory design—involving users and affected communities in technology development—produces better outcomes.

You Might Notice Problems Others Miss

People directly affected by AI systems often notice problems that others miss.

Lived Experience Reveals Edge Cases:

Developers test AI systems, but they can't anticipate every real-world scenario. Users encounter edge cases and unusual situations that reveal problems. Your report of an AI system failing in a specific context provides valuable information.

You Experience Bias Directly:

If an AI system treats you unfairly due to race, gender, age, disability, or other factors, you experience that bias directly. While developers can test for bias statistically, nothing replaces reports from people experiencing discrimination. Many discovered AI biases came from users reporting unfair treatment.

You Understand Context Developers Don't:

An AI system might technically work, but still cause problems in specific contexts. A teacher knows that an AI grading system might discourage creative writing even if it accurately scores essays. A healthcare worker knows that an efficient AI scheduling system might create problematic patient care dynamics. Context matters, and people in those contexts are experts on them.

Diverse Perspectives Improve Outcomes

Homogeneous groups make worse decisions than diverse ones, especially when it comes to technologies that affect diverse populations. This is well-established in research.

The Blind Spots of Homogeneity:

When AI is developed primarily by young men in Silicon Valley, it reflects their perspectives and misses others'. This has led to:

- Facial recognition that works poorly on women and people of color
- Voice assistants that don't understand female voices as well as male ones
- AI systems that fail to accommodate disabilities
- Health tracking that doesn't account for female biology
- Products that assume Western cultural norms

Diverse participation in conversations about AI helps catch these blind spots before they harm people.

Innovation Through Diversity:

Different perspectives don't just catch problems—they generate better ideas. Someone from a different background might envision beneficial AI applications that others wouldn't think of, or propose solutions to AI challenges that wouldn't occur to homogeneous groups.

The best outcomes come from diversity of perspectives: technical experts, ethicists, people from affected communities, policymakers, workers, and consumers all contributing their insights.

What We're All Figuring Out Together

The conversation about AI isn't about revealing answers that experts already know. We're genuinely figuring things out together because many questions don't have clear answers yet.

Questions Without Clear Answers

How much job displacement is acceptable in exchange for efficiency?

There's no objectively correct answer. Some people prioritize economic efficiency and believe displaced workers will find new opportunities. Others prioritize employment stability and community preservation. These are value judgments that society must collectively make.

Where should we draw the line between helpful personalization and manipulative targeting?

AI can personalize content to individual interests—helpful for finding relevant information, but potentially manipulative when used to exploit vulnerabilities or create addiction. Where's the line? Society is figuring this out.

How do we balance security benefits against privacy costs?

AI surveillance can catch criminals and prevent terrorism, but also enables authoritarian control and chills freedom. Different societies might reach different balances based on their values and histories. There's no universal right answer.

What transparency is required for AI decisions?

Complete transparency might reveal proprietary information or enable gaming the system. Complete opacity denies people understanding of decisions affecting them. The right balance is contested.

How do we define and measure fairness?

Mathematicians have proven that different definitions of algorithmic fairness are mutually incompatible—you can't simultaneously optimize for all of them. Choosing which definition to prioritize involves value judgments that society must make.

What should AI never be allowed to do?

Some applications of AI might be fundamentally problematic regardless of how well they're implemented. Should AI make life-or-death medical decisions? Should autonomous weapons exist? Should AI manipulate people's emotions? These boundaries must be collectively determined.

The Answers Depend on Democratic Deliberation

Because these questions involve values and trade-offs, not just technical facts, answering them requires democratic deliberation—society collectively discussing options, weighing trade-offs, and reaching decisions that reflect shared values.

This deliberation is happening now in:

- Government hearings and regulatory proceedings
- Academic research and conferences
- Corporate ethics boards and policy teams

- Civil society organizations and advocacy groups
- Media coverage and public discussion
- International bodies and standard-setting organizations

But this deliberation is incomplete without broad public participation. When conversations happen only among elites—politicians, executives, academics—they miss essential perspectives and may reach conclusions that don't reflect broader societal values.

Norms Are Being Established Now

The norms governing AI use—what's acceptable, what's not, what's expected, what's taboo—are being established right now through current practices and conversations.

First-Mover Disadvantage:

Often, whoever does something first sets the norm. If companies start using AI in privacy-invasive ways without pushback, that becomes normalized. If workers don't object to invasive AI monitoring initially, it becomes standard practice. Norms are easier to establish than to change later.

This makes current participation particularly important. The norms being set now will shape AI use for years or decades. Missing this conversation means accepting norms established by others.

Norm Cascades:

Social norms can shift suddenly when enough people begin questioning them. Smoking was normalized, then rapidly became taboo as public opinion shifted. Similar shifts could happen with AI practices—what's currently accepted could become unacceptable if public opinion turns against it.

Your participation in questioning current practices and advocating for better ones contributes to potential norm shifts.

How to Participate Effectively

Understanding that you should participate is one thing; knowing how to do so effectively is another. Here are practical ways to make your participation meaningful.

Start Where You Are

You don't need to become an AI expert or activist. Start with what's accessible:

Notice AI in Your Life:

Pay attention to where you encounter AI. When you do, ask yourself:

- How is this AI affecting me?
- Does this seem fair and beneficial?
- What concerns does this raise?
- Who benefits from this AI system?

This awareness is the foundation for informed participation.

Discuss With People You Know:

Conversations with family, friends, and colleagues about AI are valuable. They:

- Spread awareness
- Develop collective understanding
- Identify shared concerns
- Build momentum for action

These informal conversations are part of the broader social deliberation about AI.

Engage Where You Have Stakes:

Focus on AI issues in contexts where you're directly affected:

- Your workplace
- Your children's school
- Your community
- Your profession
- Your hobbies and interests

You don't need to engage with every AI issue—focusing where you have direct stakes and expertise makes participation more meaningful and sustainable.

Educate Yourself, But Don't Wait to Be an Expert

Learn Continuously:

Stay informed about AI developments through:

- Quality journalism covering AI
- Educational resources and explainer articles
- Documentaries about AI
- Community education programs
- Online courses (many free)

But you don't need to wait until you're an expert to participate. Basic understanding is sufficient for meaningful engagement.

Follow Diverse Sources:

Get information from multiple perspectives:

- Tech companies promoting AI
- Critics raising concerns about AI
- Researchers studying AI impacts
- Journalists investigating AI issues
- Civil society groups advocating for responsible AI

This balanced information helps form nuanced views.

Focus on Questions and Concerns, Not Solutions

You don't need to propose detailed policy solutions to participate meaningfully. Articulating questions and concerns is itself valuable:

Good Questions to Raise:

- "How will this AI system affect people in [specific situation]?"
- "Has this AI been tested for bias against [specific group]?"
- "What happens if this AI makes a mistake?"
- "Who benefits from this AI, and who might be harmed?"
- "What transparency exists around how this AI makes decisions?"
- "What recourse do people have if AI treats them unfairly?"

These questions push decision-makers to think carefully about AI deployment.

Valid Concerns to Express:

- "I'm worried about the privacy implications of this AI surveillance."
- "I'm concerned this AI might perpetuate discrimination."
- "I'm anxious about job displacement in my industry."
- "I'm troubled by AI-generated misinformation."
- "I'm uncomfortable with how this AI is being used."

Expressing concerns signals what matters to people and what requires attention.

Amplify Voices of Affected Communities

Sometimes the most valuable participation is amplifying others' voices, especially from communities most affected by AI but least represented in conversations about it.

Listen to Marginalized Communities:

Communities experiencing discrimination often notice AI bias first. Workers in automatable jobs understand the impacts on employment. Privacy-vulnerable populations recognize surveillance risks earliest.

Listening to these communities and elevating their concerns makes conversations more inclusive and complete.

Share Others' Stories:

If you have platforms or networks, sharing perspectives from affected communities extends their reach. Retweeting, reposting, or verbally sharing others' experiences in discussions brings diverse voices into the conversation.

Participate in Formal Processes

When opportunities arise, participate in formal processes shaping AI governance:

Submit Public Comments:

When government agencies seek public input on AI regulations, submit comments sharing your perspective. These submissions become part of the official record and influence policy.

Attend Public Meetings:

City councils, school boards, and other bodies sometimes hold meetings on AI use within their jurisdictions. Attending and speaking during public comment periods influences local decisions.

Sign Petitions and Support Advocacy:

When organizations circulate petitions about AI issues you care about, signing and sharing them demonstrates public concern to decision-makers.

Participate in Surveys and Research:

Researchers studying public opinion about AI help inform policy. Participating in surveys and studies contributes data about public perspectives.

Demand Accountability

Hold institutions accountable for their AI use:

Ask Questions of Institutions:

- Ask your employer how AI is used in hiring, evaluation, and workplace monitoring
- Ask your bank how AI affects lending decisions
- Ask your children's school about AI in education
- Ask your city government about AI surveillance
- Ask companies whose products you use about their AI practices

These questions create pressure for transparency and accountability.

Report Problems:

When AI systems behave problematically, report it:

- File complaints with appropriate agencies
- Contact the company's customer service
- Report to consumer protection organizations
- Share experiences with journalists investigating AI
- Document problems for potential collective action

Problem reports help identify issues requiring attention.

Vote With Your Attention and Support

Support Responsible Companies:

When you have choices, support companies and organizations demonstrating responsible AI development and use. Market signals matter, and companies respond to customer preferences.

Support Responsible Journalism:

Quality journalism investigating AI issues and explaining them to the public is essential infrastructure for informed public participation. Supporting such journalism (through subscriptions, donations, or sharing) strengthens this infrastructure.

Support Advocacy Organizations:

Organizations advocating for responsible AI—like the AI Now Institute, Electronic Frontier Foundation, Algorithm Justice League, and many others—need public support to be effective. Supporting them amplifies your impact beyond individual participation.

The Stakes: Why This Matters

Some might wonder whether individual participation really matters given the power of tech companies and governments. It does matter, for several reasons.

Collective Action Changes Outcomes

Individual action alone has a limited impact, but collective action changes outcomes. When many people express concerns, participate in consultations, contact representatives, and make market choices based on AI practices, it creates pressure that institutions cannot ignore.

Historical Examples:

Public pressure has changed technology development before:

- Privacy concerns led to regulations like GDPR
- Backlash against manipulative social media algorithms has pushed companies to modify features
- Worker organizing has influenced how companies deploy workplace surveillance
- Public outcry stopped specific controversial AI applications (like Amazon's facial recognition for law enforcement)

These changes happened because many people participated in expressing concerns and demanding better.

Silence Is Acceptance

If only tech companies and their advocates participate in conversations about AI, their preferences will dominate outcomes. Silence from the broader public signals acceptance of whatever those actors decide.

Participation—even just expressing concern—signals that you care about these issues and that decision-makers should consider broader perspectives. It prevents default outcomes that might not serve public interests.

Democracy Requires Participation

Democratic governance of powerful technologies requires informed public participation. If citizens don't engage with how AI is governed, governance will happen anyway—but without democratic input or accountability.

AI is too important to be left solely to corporate decision-making or technocratic governance. Democratic control requires democratic participation.

Your Participation Encourages Others

When you participate—asking questions, expressing concerns, attending meetings, staying informed—it encourages others to do likewise. Social norms around civic participation spread through modeling. Your engagement makes others more likely to engage.

Conversely, if everyone assumes someone else will handle AI governance, no one does, and we get governance by default rather than by design.

The Future Is Being Decided Now

Decisions made now about AI will shape the coming decades. The norms, regulations, and practices established in these early years of widespread AI deployment will be difficult to change later.

This makes current participation particularly consequential. Missing these conversations means accepting a future shaped entirely by others' decisions.

Conclusion: Your Voice Matters

The development and governance of AI isn't something happening to you—it's something you can participate in shaping. The decisions about how AI is developed, deployed, and governed are being made now, and they involve value judgments where your perspective is as legitimate as anyone's.

You don't need technical expertise to participate meaningfully. Your lived experience, your values, your concerns, and your questions are valuable contributions to the conversation.

We're collectively figuring out:

- What problems AI should solve
- What trade-offs are acceptable
- Where to draw ethical lines
- What transparency and accountability look like
- How to balance innovation with safety
- How to ensure AI benefits everyone
- What rules and norms should govern AI use

These aren't questions with predetermined technical answers. They're questions that society must answer collectively through democratic deliberation and participation.

Your voice is part of that deliberation. Whether you:

- Share your experiences with AI systems
- Express concerns to employers or policymakers
- Make informed consumer choices
- Participate in public comment periods
- Vote based on candidates' AI positions
- Discuss AI with your community
- Amplify voices of affected communities
- Ask questions of institutions using AI

You're participating in shaping AI's future. Each action might seem small, but collective participation creates the pressure, insight, and democratic input necessary for responsible AI development.

The alternative to broad participation is AI developed and governed by a narrow set of actors pursuing their own interests. That's a recipe for AI that serves some people well while harming others, that optimizes for profit or power over human welfare, that perpetuates existing inequities or creates new ones.

Inclusive participation—everyone affected by AI having a voice in how it develops—is how we move toward AI that genuinely benefits humanity broadly. This requires your participation. Your perspective on how AI should work in society doesn't just matter—it's essential.

The conversation about AI is happening now. You're invited to join it. In fact, you're not just invited—you're needed. The future we're building with AI depends on who participates in deciding what that future should look like. Make sure your voice is part of that conversation.

Eleven
AI Explained for Young Adults

AI is disrupting your education (can do homework), reshaping careers (some jobs disappearing, new ones emerging), and curating your social life through algorithms.

For Young Adults—AI Will Define Your Future, So Learn to Shape It

If you're in high school or college right now, AI isn't just another technology you'll learn to use—it's the defining force that will shape your education, career, relationships, and the entire world you'll inherit as an adult. Understanding AI isn't optional anymore; it's as essential as reading, writing, and critical thinking. Your generation will either be shaped by AI or shape AI. Which one depends on the choices you make starting right now.

AI Is Already Rewriting the Rules of Education

Let's be direct: AI has fundamentally changed what education means, and you're experiencing this disruption in real time.

The Homework Crisis:

Tools like ChatGPT can write your essays, solve your math problems, code your programming assignments, and complete virtually any traditional homework in seconds. This creates an unprecedented challenge: what does learning mean when AI can do the assignments meant to teach you?

You're facing questions no previous generation encountered:

- Is using ChatGPT for homework cheating or just using available tools, like calculators?
- If AI can write essays, why are you still being taught to write essays?
- How do teachers fairly assess learning when they can't tell if work is yours or AI's?
- What skills actually matter if machines can handle so much cognitive work?

Different Schools, Different Rules:

Right now, there's no consensus. Some of your teachers completely ban AI, treating it like plagiarism. Others encourage it as a learning tool. Still others haven't figured out their position yet. This inconsistency is frustrating, but it reflects a genuine dilemma: we're all figuring this out together.

Here's the Uncomfortable Truth:

You can use AI to get through school without learning much. You can have it write your papers, solve your problems, and complete your assignments. You might even get good grades. But you'd be cheating yourself far more than you're cheating the system.

The skills you develop now—critical thinking, problem-solving, writing clearly, analyzing information—are what will distinguish you in an AI world. If you outsource all of that to AI during your formative years, you'll enter adulthood without the capabilities that make you valuable, interesting, and effective.

A Smarter Approach:

Use AI as a learning tool, not a replacement for learning:

Good uses:

- Having AI explain concepts you don't understand
- Using it to generate practice problems
- Getting feedback on your rough drafts
- Exploring different approaches to a problem
- Overcoming writer's block or getting started
- Learning how to phrase questions more effectively

Bad uses:

- Having AI write entire assignments, you just submit
- Using it to avoid engaging with difficult material
- Letting it do the thinking you should be doing
- Copying its output without understanding it

The difference: In good uses, AI helps you learn and improve. In bad uses, AI prevents you from learning and makes you dependent on it.

Why This Actually Matters to Your Future:

When you enter the workforce, you'll work alongside people who genuinely developed their skills and people who outsourced their learning to AI. The difference will be obvious. Those with real capabilities will advance, lead, innovate, and earn more. Those who over-relied on AI will struggle because they never developed the underlying competencies.

You're essentially deciding right now: do you want to be capable and valuable, or dependent and mediocre? AI makes mediocrity easier to achieve, but that's not an advantage—it's a trap.

Assessment Is Changing:

Because of AI, education is adapting. Expect to see:

- More in-class assessments where AI isn't available
- Oral examinations where you explain your thinking
- Project-based work focused on application, not just knowledge
- Collaborative assignments that require genuine human interaction
- Assessments of your process, not just your final product
- Greater emphasis on creativity, judgment, and uniquely human skills

These changes might seem harder than traditional homework, but they're actually preparing you better for a world where AI handles routine cognitive work, and humans focus on what machines can't do.

Your Career Will Be Fundamentally Different

By the time you're in your thirties and forties, the job market will look radically different from what it does today. AI is changing not just specific jobs but the entire nature of work.

Jobs That Are Changing or Disappearing:

Be realistic about careers being disrupted by AI. Jobs involving routine, predictable tasks are significantly impacted:

- Routine data entry and processing (already mostly automated)
- Basic bookkeeping and tax preparation (AI handles most of this)
- Simple customer service (chatbots increasingly handle this)
- Routine legal document preparation (AI drafts contracts and briefs)
- Basic translation work (AI translates well enough for most purposes)

- Simple writing and content creation (AI generates articles, marketing copy)
- Some aspects of radiology and pathology (AI reads medical images accurately)
- Entry-level programming (AI writes code from descriptions)
- Basic graphic design (AI generates logos and layouts)
- Certain financial analysis roles (AI analyzes markets and data)

This doesn't mean these entire professions disappear; it means they transform dramatically. The routine parts get automated, and humans focus on complex, judgment-heavy aspects.

Jobs Being Created:

AI also creates entirely new career categories:

- AI ethics specialists (ensuring AI is used responsibly)
- AI trainers (teaching AI systems new capabilities)
- Prompt engineers (people skilled at communicating with AI effectively)
- AI auditors (checking systems for bias and fairness)
- Human-AI interaction designers (making AI usable for people)
- Synthetic media detection specialists (identifying deepfakes)
- AI safety researchers (preventing dangerous AI applications)
- Personal AI curators (helping people manage their AI tools)
- AI-assisted creativity directors (combining human vision with AI capabilities)

Many of these didn't exist five years ago. Many more will emerge that we can't predict yet.

The Skills That Will Actually Matter

Focus relentlessly on developing capabilities that AI struggles with:

Creativity and Innovation: AI can recombine existing ideas, but it struggles with genuinely novel thinking. Your ability to imagine new possibilities, connect unrelated concepts, and envision what doesn't exist yet will be invaluable. Creative work—whether in arts, business, science, or any field—will remain distinctly human.

Emotional Intelligence: Understanding people, reading social situations, building relationships, leading teams, motivating others, negotiating conflicts—these require emotional intelligence that AI fundamentally lacks. As AI handles more technical work, human interaction skills become more valuable, not less.

Complex Judgment: AI can process data and identify patterns, but making judgments in ambiguous situations with incomplete information, ethical complexity, and high stakes—that's where humans excel. Learning to make good decisions with uncertainty will distinguish you.

Ethical Reasoning: As AI systems make more decisions, someone needs to determine if those decisions are right, fair, and aligned with human values. People who can navigate ethical complexity will be essential in an AI world.

Adaptability and Learning: The specific knowledge you gain now will become outdated. The ability to learn new things quickly, adapt to change, and stay relevant as fields evolve matters more than any specific skill set. Cultivate learning itself as your core competency.

Cross-Disciplinary Thinking: AI often operates within domains. Humans excel at connecting ideas across different fields. The ability to integrate knowledge from technology, humanities, arts, sciences, and business creates unique value.

Communication: Whether explaining complex ideas clearly, telling compelling stories, persuading others, or facilitating understanding across different perspectives—communication skills matter enormously. AI generates text, but meaningful human communication involves more than words.

Collaboration: Working effectively with diverse people on complex problems requires skills AI doesn't have—building trust, managing group dynamics, resolving conflicts, and co-creating solutions. Develop these capabilities.

Critical Thinking: As AI generates more content and information, the ability to evaluate what's true, identify bias, recognize manipulation, and think independently becomes crucial. Don't let AI do your thinking for you—develop strong analytical capabilities.

Technical Literacy (But Not Necessarily Programming): You need to understand AI well enough to use it effectively, question its outputs, recognize its limitations, and work alongside it. This doesn't necessarily mean becoming a programmer or data scientist—it means becoming an informed, capable user and evaluator of AI systems.

The Meta-Skill: Learning to Work With AI

Perhaps most important: learn to work effectively with AI. This means:

- Understanding what AI is good at and what it's not
- Knowing when to use AI and when human work is better
- Being able to prompt AI systems effectively
- Critically evaluating AI outputs rather than blindly accepting them
- Combining AI capabilities with human judgment
- Using AI to enhance your work, not replace your thinking

Think of AI as a powerful tool, like a car. You don't need to understand how the engine works to drive effectively, but you do need to know how to control it, when to use it instead of walking, and how to handle it responsibly. Similarly with AI.

Your Social Life and Relationships Are AI-Mediated

Your generation is the first to grow up with social lives fundamentally shaped by AI algorithms, and this has profound implications you should understand.

The Algorithm Is Curating Your Reality:

Every social media platform you use—Instagram, TikTok, YouTube, Twitter/X, Facebook, Snapchat—uses AI to determine what you see. These algorithms aren't neutral; they're optimized for engagement, which means showing you content that keeps you scrolling, even if that content isn't good for you.

How This Affects You:

Filter Bubbles: AI shows you more of what you engage with, which can trap you in echo chambers where you only see perspectives you already agree with. This feels comfortable, but it limits your understanding of different viewpoints and can make you less capable of engaging with people who think differently.

Mental Health Impact: AI algorithms have learned that content triggering strong emotions—envy, outrage, anxiety, excitement—keeps people engaged. So they amplify such content. Studies link heavy social media use to increased anxiety, depression, and poor self-esteem, especially among young people.

Comparison Culture: AI shows you highlight reels of others' lives—carefully curated, filtered, edited versions of reality. Constant exposure to this creates unhealthy comparisons and unrealistic standards. Remember: you're comparing your full reality to others' best moments.

Distorted Politics: Political content that's outrageous or extreme gets amplified because it generates engagement. This can make politics seem more polarized than they actually are and can radicalize people by feeding them increasingly extreme content.

What You Can Do:

Consciously Diversify: Actively follow people with different perspectives. Seek out content that challenges your views. Don't let the algorithm trap you in a bubble.

Set Boundaries: Limit social media time. Notice how different platforms affect your mood and well-being. Take breaks when needed. Your mental health matters more than staying constantly connected.

Reality Check: Remind yourself that social media isn't reality. It's a curated performance. Others aren't as happy, successful, or perfect as they appear online. You're not behind; you're just seeing unrealistic comparisons.

Engage Meaningfully: Focus on genuine connections rather than performance. Message friends directly rather than just consuming their posts. Build real relationships, not just online personas.

AI and Dating:

Many of you will meet romantic partners through dating apps that use AI to match you. Be aware:

The Algorithm's Incentives: Dating apps profit by keeping you using the app, not necessarily by finding you a great match quickly. The AI is optimized for engagement, which sometimes conflicts with finding you lasting love.

Authenticity Matters: AI can write your messages, choose your photos, even generate your profile. But relationships require genuine human connection. Using too much AI in dating can attract people who like the AI-enhanced version of you, not the real you.

The Paradox of Choice: AI presents you with seemingly endless options, which research shows can make people less satisfied with their choices and less committed to relationships. More options don't necessarily mean better outcomes.

The Information Crisis You're Inheriting

Your generation faces an information environment unlike any in human history, and it's getting worse.

Deepfakes and Synthetic Media:

AI can now create videos of people saying things they never said, photos of events that never happened, and audio in anyone's voice saying anything.

Documents can look completely authentic. As this technology improves, distinguishing real from fake will become nearly impossible without specialized tools. By the time you're voting in major elections, candidates could be shown in completely fabricated videos doing or saying outrageous things, released too close to election day to be effectively debunked.

AI-Generated Content Flood:

Much of the content online is already AI-generated—articles, social media posts, comments, reviews, images. This percentage is rapidly increasing. Soon, most content online might be synthetic.

Why This Matters:

- Product reviews might be fake
- News articles might be fabricated
- Social movements might be AI-generated astroturfing
- Historical "evidence" might be manufactured
- Scientific papers might be AI-written with fabricated data

What You Can Do:

Develop Media Literacy:

- Always consider the source—who created this and why?
- Cross-check important information across multiple reliable sources
- Be especially skeptical of content designed to trigger strong emotions
- Learn to recognize signs of AI generation (though this gets harder)
- Understand that seeing something online doesn't make it real

Verify Before Sharing:

- Don't spread information you haven't verified
- Check facts before sharing outrageous claims
- Use fact-checking resources
- Understand that sharing misinformation harms others even if you didn't create it

Support Quality Information:

- Subscribe to or support legitimate journalism
- Value sources that verify information rather than just aggregating it
- Recognize that quality information costs money to produce

- Be willing to pay for trustworthy sources

This Is Your Problem:

Previous generations grew up with relatively trustworthy information sources—major newspapers, network news, and established encyclopedias. You're growing up in an environment where information is abundant, but trustworthiness is scarce. This isn't fair, but it's reality. You need to develop skills for navigating this environment that previous generations didn't need.

Privacy: You're Trading It Away Without Realizing

Your generation is often more comfortable sharing information online than previous ones, but you might not fully grasp what you're giving up.

What's Actually Being Collected:

Companies collect enormous amounts of data about you:

- Every search query you type
- Every post you like, share, or comment on
- Every video you watch and for how long
- Every location your phone visits
- Every purchase you make online
- Every message you send on many platforms
- Every website you visit
- Your contacts, photos, and calendar
- Your voice (if you use voice assistants)
- Your face (through facial recognition)

How It's Used:

This data doesn't just sit in databases. It's used to:

Train AI Systems: Your photos train facial recognition. Your writing trains language AI. Your behavior trains recommendation systems. You're effectively working for free to train AI that companies profit from.

Create Detailed Profiles: AI analyzes all this data to create psychological profiles of you—your personality, preferences, vulnerabilities, fears, desires, political views, health status, financial situation, and more. These profiles are incredibly accurate.

Target You: These profiles enable micro-targeted advertising, content, and potentially manipulation. AI can identify your vulnerabilities and exploit them to sell products, spread propaganda, or influence your behavior.

Make Decisions About You: Future employers might use AI to analyze your social media and decide whether to hire you. Lenders might use it to determine if you qualify for loans. Insurance companies might use it to set rates. Landlords might use it to decide if you can rent an apartment.

Surveillance: In some countries, governments use this data for social control and surveillance. Even in democracies, government agencies can access much of this data with warrants or, in some cases, without.

The Long-Term Implications:

Everything you post now will exist essentially forever. Your future employers, romantic partners, children, and even grandchildren might see posts you make today. AI makes this information searchable and analyzable in ways that weren't possible before.

That drunken photo, that angry rant, that controversial opinion, that embarrassing moment—it could all resurface years or decades later when context is lost, and consequences are different.

You Have More Control Than You Think:

Adjust Privacy Settings: Most apps and services have privacy settings you can tighten. Take time to review and adjust them. Default settings are usually the most permissive.

Be Selective About Sharing: Before posting, ask: "Would I be okay with this being seen by future employers, family members, or even being shown on the news?" If not, don't post it.

Use Privacy-Focused Alternatives: Some apps and services prioritize privacy. Signal instead of WhatsApp for messaging. DuckDuckGo instead of Google for searching. Firefox with privacy extensions instead of Chrome for browsing.

Read Before Clicking "Accept": Yes, the terms of service are long, but at least skim them to understand what you're agreeing to. Many times, you're agreeing to extensive data collection and use.

Exercise Your Rights: In some places (like Europe with GDPR, California with CCPA), you have legal rights to access your data, correct it, delete it, or restrict its use. Exercise these rights.

The Fundamental Trade-Off:

"Free" services aren't actually free—you're paying with your data and attention. Sometimes that's a fair trade, but make it consciously, not by default.

You Will Determine What AI Becomes

Here's the empowering message: your generation will ultimately determine what role AI plays in society.

You'll Be Making the Decisions:

In 10-20 years, people your age will be:

- Legislators writing AI regulations
- Executives deciding how companies use AI
- Researchers developing new AI capabilities
- Judges ruling on AI-related cases
- Journalists covering AI developments
- Activists advocating for responsible AI
- Teachers educating the next generation about AI
- Parents deciding what AI their children can use

The choices you make will shape AI's future far more than anything previous generations have done.

Prepare Now:

Educate Yourself Deeply: Don't settle for surface-level understanding. Really learn how AI works, what it can and can't do, and what the important questions are. This doesn't necessarily mean studying computer science (though you could), but it means becoming genuinely informed.

Develop Strong Opinions: Think critically about AI's role in society. What applications are beneficial? What's harmful? Where should we draw lines? What values should guide AI development? Form informed opinions you can articulate and defend.

Participate in the Conversation: Discuss AI with friends, family, teachers. Write about it. Engage in online discussions. Attend talks and forums. Make your voice heard. The conversation about AI is happening now, and your generation's perspective is essential.

Consider AI-Related Careers: Whether directly (AI engineering, policy, ethics) or indirectly (any field that will be shaped by AI—which is most of them), consider how you can influence AI's development and use.

Your Values Can Reshape AI:

Previous generations built social media optimized for engagement and profit, often at the expense of user well-being. Your generation can choose different priorities:

- Well-being over engagement
- Privacy over data extraction
- Fairness over efficiency
- Transparency over opacity
- Human connection over algorithmic matching
- Truth over virality

But this only happens if you actively push for these values in the systems you build, support, and use.

The Biggest Risk: Passivity

Perhaps the greatest danger for your generation isn't that AI will be misused—it's that you'll be passive about it.

Passive Looks Like:

- Using whatever AI tools companies provide without questioning them
- Accepting whatever AI shows you as reality
- Letting AI make decisions without understanding how
- Consuming AI-generated content without critical thought
- Allowing AI to atrophy your own capabilities
- Accepting AI's role in society as inevitable and unchangeable

Active Looks Like:

- Questioning how AI works and what its incentives are
- Critically evaluating AI outputs rather than accepting them
- Demanding transparency and accountability in AI systems
- Developing strong capabilities AI can't replicate
- Using AI as a tool that enhances your work, not replaces your thinking
- Participating in shaping AI's development and governance

The passive path is easier in the short term, but leads to a future where AI shapes you rather than you shaping it. The active path requires effort but leads to a future where AI serves your values and interests.

Don't Face This Alone

Navigating AI can feel overwhelming, but remember:

Your Entire Generation Is Figuring This Out: You're not alone in feeling uncertain, overwhelmed, or conflicted about AI. These are complex issues without simple answers, and everyone your age is grappling with them.

Talk to Each Other: Discuss AI with friends. Share concerns, strategies, and insights. Figure out together how to navigate an AI-shaped world. Collective wisdom exceeds individual understanding.

Learn from Older Generations: While adults might not fully understand AI, they've navigated previous technological disruptions. Their experience adapting to personal computers, the internet, and social media offers a valuable perspective on managing technological change.

Trust Your Instincts: You understand aspects of AI that older generations don't because you've grown up with it. If something about AI feels wrong or concerning to you, that instinct is worth listening to and exploring.

It's Okay to Make Mistakes: Nobody has this figured out perfectly. You'll sometimes use AI unwisely, share things you shouldn't, or trust AI when you shouldn't. That's part of learning. What matters is learning from mistakes and adjusting.

The Bottom Line for Young Adults

AI isn't something that will affect your future—it's affecting your present and will be central to your entire adult life. You can't avoid it, and trying to would be counterproductive. But you also shouldn't passively accept whatever AI systems are built and deployed.

Your Path Forward:

Understand It: Develop a genuine, deep understanding of AI—not just what it is, but how it works, what it can't do, what questions it raises.

Develop Irreplaceable Skills: Focus relentlessly on capabilities that make you valuable in an AI world—creativity, judgment, emotional intelligence, ethical reasoning, critical thinking, complex problem-solving.

Use It Wisely: Employ AI as a tool that enhances your capabilities, not as a replacement for developing your own. Let it handle routine tasks so you can focus on higher-level thinking; don't let it do your thinking for you.

Question It: Don't accept AI outputs, recommendations, or decisions without critical evaluation. Understand that AI systems have biases, limitations, and misaligned incentives.

Protect Yourself: Guard your privacy, verify information, be aware of manipulation, and maintain boundaries with technology.

Shape It: Participate actively in determining AI's role in society. Your generation will make decisions that determine whether AI primarily benefits or harms humanity.

Stay Human: In an increasingly AI-mediated world, maintain genuine human connections, authentic expression, and values-driven decision-making.

The Choice Is Yours

Your generation faces a choice no previous generation confronted: will you be passive subjects of AI systems built by others, or active shapers of an AI future aligned with your values?

The passive path is easy. Use the AI tools provided. Accept the content that the algorithms show you. Let AI handle thinking and creating. Don't question how systems work or what incentives drive them. Take the path of least resistance. This leads to a world where AI optimizes for whatever tech companies and governments decide to optimize for, and you adapt to whatever role is left for humans.

The active path is harder. Develop real capabilities. Think critically. Question systems. Demand better. Participate in governance. Build and support AI that serves human flourishing, not just profit. This leads to a world where AI is a tool serving human values, enhancing human capabilities, and directed by people who understand it deeply and use it wisely.

Which path will you choose?

That decision, multiplied across your entire generation, will determine the future of AI and humanity's relationship with it. The stakes couldn't be higher. The opportunity couldn't be greater.

The future isn't happening to you—you're creating it. AI is the most powerful tool your generation will wield. The question is: will you wield it consciously and responsibly, or will you let it wield you?

Twelve
For the Novice or Elderly
AI Can Help You

You're not too new or too old for AI—you don't need technical expertise, just basic know-how (like driving without understanding engines). AI already helps through your phone, email spam filters, and GPS.

If you're new to AI or an older Millennial, Gen X or Boomer, AI might seem like just another confusing technology change in a world that's already moved too fast. You might feel left behind, intimidated, or convinced that AI is something for younger people while you're too old to understand or benefit from it. None of this is true. AI can genuinely help you live better, more independently, and more connected—and your perspective on how society should use AI matters deeply. Let me explain why and how.

You're Not Too Green or Old, and It's Not Too Complicated

First, let's address the fear that might be your biggest barrier: the belief that you're too green or old to understand or use AI, or that technology has passed you by.

Your Brain Works Fine:

The idea that adults can't learn new things is a harmful myth. Yes, learning might take more practice than it did when you were 18, but your brain remains fully capable of learning throughout your life. In fact, in many ways, your mature brain has advantages:

Experience: You've lived through enormous technological changes—perhaps television becoming common, computers entering homes, the internet connecting the world, and smartphones becoming ubiquitous. You've adapted before; you can adapt again.

Judgment: Your life experience gives you better judgment about what matters and what doesn't. You're less likely than younger people to get caught up in technology for its own sake and are better at evaluating whether something actually improves your life.

Wisdom: You understand what makes life meaningful—relationships, purpose, contribution. This wisdom helps you use technology as a tool for what matters rather than letting it dominate your life.

Perspective: Having seen previous technologies arrive with both promises and problems, you're less likely to be either unrealistically utopian or unnecessarily fearful about AI.

You Don't Need to Understand How It Works:

Just like you don't need to understand how a car engine works to drive, or how electricity works to use a light switch, you don't need to understand AI's technical details to benefit from it.

What matters is understanding:

- What AI tools are available
- What they can help you do
- How to use them basically
- When to be cautious

Think of AI like an automatic transmission in a car. Someone had to understand the complex engineering to build it, but you just need to know "D" for drive and "R" for reverse. Similarly with AI—you need basic operational knowledge, not engineering expertise.

AI Is Already Helping You (Probably Without You Knowing)

You might already be using AI without realizing it, which proves you can handle it:

- **If You Use a Smartphone:**
  - **Voice Assistants:** When you say "Hey Siri" or "Okay Google" and ask a question—"What's the weather?" "Call my daughter." "Set a timer for 20 minutes."—that's AI understanding your voice, figuring out what you want, and taking action. You're using sophisticated AI by just talking naturally.
  - **Predictive Text:** When you type a text message, and your phone suggests the next word, that's AI predicting what you want to say based on patterns in language. It helps you type faster with less effort.
  - **Facial Recognition:** If your phone unlocks when it sees your face, that's AI recognizing you among billions of possible people, instantly and accurately.
  - **Photo Organization:** If your phone automatically groups photos by person or organizes them by place or date, AI is doing that. It's recognizing faces, locations, and even what's in the photos (beaches, mountains, pets, food) without you labeling anything.
- **If You Use Email:**
  - **Spam Filtering:** The reason your email inbox isn't flooded with thousands of junk emails is AI identifying and blocking spam before you see it. It's working constantly in the background, protecting you.
- **If You Watch TV or Movies:**
  - **Recommendations:** When Netflix suggests shows you might like, or YouTube recommends videos, that's AI that's learned your preferences from what you've watched before. It's like having someone who knows your taste helping you find entertainment.

- **If You Use GPS or Navigation:**
  - **Route Planning:** When Google Maps or your car's GPS suggests the fastest route, predicts arrival times, and warns about traffic, that's AI analyzing data from millions of drivers to help you avoid delays.
- **If You Bank Online:**
  - **Fraud Detection:** AI monitors your accounts for suspicious activity—purchases in unusual places, odd spending patterns, potential identity theft. It's like having a security guard watching your money 24/7.

You're already successfully using AI in all these ways. This proves you're capable of using it; you just might not have known these tools were AI.

How AI Can Specifically Help You

Beyond what you might already use, AI offers tools that can be particularly helpful as we age:

Health and Safety:

Medical Monitoring: Smartwatches and medical devices with AI can:

- Monitor your heart and detect irregular rhythms that might indicate atrial fibrillation (a serious condition)
- Detect if you fall and automatically call for help
- Track your activity and sleep patterns
- Remind you to take medications on schedule
- Monitor blood sugar if you're diabetic
- Track blood pressure trends

Some of these devices have literally saved lives by detecting heart problems early or calling emergency services after falls.

Medication Management: AI apps can:

- Send reminders when it's time to take medication
- Alert you if you might have missed a dose
- Warn about potential drug interactions
- Remind you to refill prescriptions
- Track your medication schedule if you take multiple pills

This is especially helpful if you take several medications at different times.

Telehealth: AI helps make virtual doctor visits work better:

- Scheduling appointments automatically
- Preparing your medical history for the doctor
- Transcribing appointments so you can review what was said
- Following up with reminders about what the doctor recommended

This is particularly valuable if mobility issues make it difficult to get to the doctor's office.

Staying Connected:

Easy Communication: AI makes staying in touch with family easier:

Voice Control: You can call family members just by saying "Call my son" or "Call Sarah" without navigating menus or typing.

Video Calling: Apps like FaceTime, Zoom, or WhatsApp use AI to improve video and audio quality so you can see and hear grandchildren clearly, even with slower internet connections.

Email Organization: AI can prioritize emails from family and friends so you see them first, while filtering out less important messages.

Photo Sharing: When family members share photos, AI can automatically organize them by person or event, making it easy to see pictures of grandchildren without searching through hundreds of photos.

Social Connection: Some AI systems are specifically designed to combat senior loneliness:

- AI companions that can have conversations when you want company
- Reminder systems that prompt you to call friends or family
- Virtual attendance at family events if you can't be there physically

While AI can't replace human connection, it can supplement it, especially for seniors living alone or far from family.

Daily Living:

Voice Control for Your Home: AI voice assistants can control your home environment:

- "Turn on the lights" (without getting up or fumbling for switches)
- "Make it warmer" (adjusting the thermostat)
- "Play some music" (entertainment without complex controls)
- "What's on my calendar today?" (checking appointments)
- "Add milk to my shopping list" (keeping track of what you need)

This is particularly helpful if mobility, vision, or arthritis make traditional controls difficult.

Reading Assistance: AI can help if reading becomes harder:

- Text-to-speech can read articles, books, or emails aloud
- AI can make text larger or adjust contrast for better visibility

- Voice assistants can read news or weather without you needing to look at screens

Reminders and Organization: AI can help with memory:

- Reminding you of appointments
- Alerting you when bills are due
- Remembering where you saved important documents
- Keeping track of birthdays and anniversaries
- Reminding you of daily tasks or routines

Transportation:

Ride Services: Apps like Uber or Lyft use AI to:

- Match you with drivers automatically
- Calculate fares
- Provide estimated arrival times
- Track your ride so family knows you arrived safely
- Store payment information so you don't handle cash

This provides independence for those who can no longer drive or prefer not to.

Autonomous Vehicles: While not widely available yet, self-driving cars are being developed specifically with seniors in mind. In the future, they could provide transportation for those who can't drive, maintaining independence.

Managing Finances:

Fraud Protection: AI monitors for scams targeting seniors:

- Detecting suspicious transactions
- Warning about potential scams

- Identifying phishing emails
- Protecting against identity theft

Unfortunately, seniors are often targeted by scammers, and AI provides a layer of protection.

Financial Management: AI can:

- Track spending and identify unusual patterns
- Help budget by categorizing expenses
- Remind you of bills to avoid late fees
- Alert you to subscription charges you might have forgotten about

Entertainment and Learning:

Personalized Content: AI suggests:

- TV shows and movies matching your interests
- Music from eras you love
- Audiobooks on topics you care about
- News articles about subjects you follow

Lifelong Learning: AI enables learning new things:

- Online courses with AI tutors
- Language learning apps that adapt to your pace
- History, science, or art content explained clearly
- Hobbies and skills taught step-by-step

Retirement is an opportunity to learn things you never had time for, and AI can facilitate that.

How to Get Started (Without Feeling Overwhelmed)

If you're interested in using AI but don't know where to start, here's a practical approach:

Start With One Thing:

Don't try to use every AI feature available. Pick one specific thing that would genuinely improve your life:

- Maybe medication reminders if you take several pills.
- Maybe voice commands if you have arthritis, making buttons difficult.
- Maybe video calling to see grandchildren.
- Maybe fall detection if you live alone.
- Maybe asking the weather and news by voice.

Master that one thing before adding more. Success with one feature builds confidence for trying others.

Ask Family for Help:

Your children or grandchildren likely enjoy helping you with technology —it's a way to connect across generations and a chance for them to feel helpful. Don't be embarrassed to ask:

- "Can you show me how to use voice commands?"
- "Can you set up video calling so I can see the grandkids?"
- "Can you help me understand this medication reminder app?"

Often, they're happy to help and might even set up features you didn't know existed.

Take a Class:

Many resources exist specifically for seniors learning technology:

- **Libraries** often offer free technology classes
- **Senior centers** frequently have computer and smartphone training
- **Community colleges** offer inexpensive courses
- **Apple Stores** provide free training for iPhone and iPad users
- **Online tutorials** on YouTube demonstrate features step-by-step (your family can help you find these)

These classes move at a pace appropriate for seniors and are taught by people who understand you're learning something new. Everyone in the class is in the same boat, which makes it less intimidating.

Use Simple Interfaces First:

Some AI tools are specifically designed to be simple and senior-friendly:

- Large-button phones with voice control.
- Simplified tablets with just essential apps.
- Medical alert systems with easy one-button operation.
- Voice assistants that require only speaking, no typing or tapping.

Start with these simpler interfaces rather than trying to master complex systems. As you get comfortable, you can always add more sophisticated tools.

Practice With Patience:

Learning new technology takes practice. You might need to:

- Try something several times before it feels natural.
- Write down the steps until you remember them.

- Ask the same questions multiple times (that's normal!).
- Make mistakes and learn from them.

Remember: Every person who now uses these tools confidently was once a beginner, too. There's no shame in taking time to learn.

Find a "Technology Buddy":

If you have a friend who's already comfortable with technology, they can be invaluable:

- You can learn together.
- They can show you what they've figured out.
- You can troubleshoot problems together.
- It's less intimidating than asking younger family members.

Many seniors find peer learning more comfortable than being taught by grandchildren.

Important Cautions: Protecting Yourself

While AI can help you, you should also be aware of risks, particularly scams targeting seniors.

AI Voice Cloning Scams:

This is perhaps the most dangerous new scam. Criminals use AI to clone voices from short recordings they find online or from public sources. Then they call seniors pretending to be grandchildren in trouble.

How It Works: You receive a call. The voice sounds exactly like your grandson. He's crying, says he's been in an accident or arrested, needs bail money urgently, and begs you not to tell his parents because he's embarrassed. He asks you to wire money immediately.

It sounds exactly like him because AI has cloned his voice. But it's not him—it's a scammer using AI.

How to Protect Yourself:

- If you get such a call, stay calm.
- Hang up immediately.
- Call your grandchild or their parents directly using a number you know is real (not the number that just called you).
- Never wire money or send gift cards based on urgent phone calls.
- Have a family code word that only real family members know, for verifying identity in emergencies.

This scam is becoming more common and is frighteningly convincing because the voice really sounds like your loved one.

AI-Generated Phishing Emails:

Scammers use AI to write convincing emails that look like they're from:

- Your bank asking you to verify account information.
- The IRS claiming you owe taxes.
- Medicare saying there's a problem with your benefits.
- Amazon saying there's an issue with your account.
- Publishers Clearing House saying you've won something.

How to Protect Yourself:

- Never click links in unexpected emails.
- Don't give personal information via email.
- Call companies directly using phone numbers from your statements or their official websites, not numbers in emails.

- Remember: Real banks, government agencies, and legitimate companies won't ask for passwords, Social Security numbers, or account information via email.
- If an offer seems too good to be true (you've won something, received an inheritance, etc.), it's a scam.

AI Customer Service Scams:

Scammers create fake customer service numbers and chatbots. You search online for customer service for your bank or a company, and the scammer's fake number or website appears in search results. When you call or chat, AI handles the interaction, seeming legitimate while stealing your information.

How to Protect Yourself:

- Don't use phone numbers from internet searches
- Use numbers on your credit card, statements, or official correspondence
- Go directly to official websites (type them in, don't click search results) for customer service information
- Be suspicious if "customer service" asks for full account numbers or passwords—real representatives can verify your identity without this

General AI Scam Principles:

- **Urgency is a red flag:** Scammers create false urgency ("act now or your account will be closed!"). Legitimate businesses give you time to respond.
- **Verify independently:** If someone contacts you claiming to be from a company or a family member, verify through a different method (calling them back at a known number).
- **Never give information to incoming contacts:** If someone

calls or emails you asking for information, don't provide it. Instead, contact the organization independently.
- **Trust your instincts:** If something feels wrong, it probably is. Better to be overcautious than scammed.

Your Privacy and AI

AI systems collect data, and you should be aware of what's being gathered and how to protect yourself.

What's Being Collected:

If you use smartphones, smart home devices, or online services, data about you might include:

- Your location and movements.
- Your voice (if you use voice assistants).
- Your photos (for facial recognition and organization).
- Your web browsing and searches.
- Your contacts and communication patterns.
- Your health data (if you use fitness trackers or medical devices).

Why This Matters:

This data is used to:

- Provide personalized services (which can be helpful).
- Target advertising to you.
- Train AI systems.
- Sometimes sold to other companies.

For most seniors, the tradeoff of some data collection for useful services is acceptable. But you should be aware and make informed choices.

How to Protect Your Privacy:

Review Privacy Settings:

- Most devices and apps have privacy settings you can adjust.
- You can typically limit what data is collected or shared.
- Ask family to help review these settings if they're confusing.
- You don't have to accept default settings—you can customize.

Be Selective About Voice Assistants:

- Voice assistants sometimes record conversations even when you didn't intend to activate them.
- You can review and delete these recordings.
- You can turn off voice assistants in rooms where you value privacy (like bedrooms).
- You can mute them when you want privacy.

Control Camera Access:

- Don't put cameras in private spaces like bedrooms or bathrooms.
- Cover laptop cameras when not in use if you're concerned.
- Review what devices have camera access in your settings.

Be Thoughtful About Sharing:

- Not every device needs access to your location.
- Not every app needs access to your contacts.
- You can deny permissions for features you don't use.

Medical Privacy:

- Medical devices and apps should comply with HIPAA (health privacy laws).

- Understand who can see your health data.
- Be cautious about health apps that aren't from established medical providers.

The Bottom Line:

Some data collection enables helpful AI features. The question is finding a balance you're comfortable with. You don't have to choose between privacy and convenience—you can have some of both with thoughtful settings.

You Don't Have to Use Every Feature

Here's something important to remember: you don't need to use every AI feature available. Technology should serve you, not the other way around.

It's Okay to:

- Use only the features that genuinely help you.
- Ignore features that seem complicated or unnecessary.
- Prefer talking to real people over AI chatbots.
- Choose simpler technology over feature-rich but complex systems.
- Take your time adopting new technology.
- Decide certain technologies aren't for you.

You're In Control:

Many seniors feel pressure to use technology because everyone else is, or because their family pushes them. But you get to decide what works for your life:

- If AI medication reminders help you, use them
- If voice control makes your home easier to manage, embrace it

- If you prefer traditional methods for something, that's fine too
- If a technology creates more frustration than benefit, don't use it

The goal is to improve your life, not to use technology for its own sake.

Your Perspective on AI Matters to Society

Beyond using AI personally, your perspective on how society should use AI is valuable and important. Don't let anyone suggest that because you're older, your opinion doesn't count.

You Have Wisdom About What Matters:

Having lived through decades of change, you understand:

- What makes life meaningful (relationships, purpose, contribution)
- What's gained and lost when technology changes society
- The importance of human connection versus convenience
- How previous technologies brought both benefits and problems
- That not all "progress" is actually progress

This wisdom is essential for making good decisions about AI. Young technologists building AI often lack this long-term perspective.

You Represent an Important Constituency:

Seniors are a large, growing portion of the population. How AI affects older adults—in healthcare, social connection, independence, fraud protection—matters enormously. But these concerns only get addressed if seniors speak up.

If AI systems are designed only by and for young people, they'll miss important needs and concerns of older adults. Your voice ensures AI serves all generations, not just the young.

Your Concerns Are Legitimate:

If you're worried about:

- AI replacing human healthcare providers
- Losing privacy to monitoring systems
- Technology making life more complicated rather than simpler
- Younger generations losing important human skills
- AI being used to exploit vulnerable seniors

These concerns deserve to be heard and addressed. Don't let anyone dismiss them as "not understanding technology." Often, concerns from people who've seen previous technologies' long-term effects prove to be well-founded.

How to Make Your Voice Heard:

Talk to Family: Share your perspectives with children and grandchildren. They need to hear from seniors about what matters as AI shapes society.

Participate in Community Discussions: When your town, senior center, or community organizations discuss technology, attend and speak up. Your experience and perspective matter.

Contact Representatives: If AI policies concern you, contact local, state, or national representatives. They need to hear from seniors about how policies affect you.

Join Senior Organizations: Groups like AARP increasingly address technology issues. Joining and participating amplifies senior voices.

Share Your Experience: If AI systems work well for you, share that. If they fail you, report it. Feedback from actual users, especially seniors, is valuable for improving these systems.

You've Adapted Before; You Can Adapt Again

If you're feeling overwhelmed by AI, remember your history of adapting to change. Depending on your age, you've lived through the introduction of television (from radio to visual media), the space age, computers (from "computers fill entire rooms" to "computers in your pocket"), the internet (from letters taking days to instant email), mobile phones (from rotary phones attached to walls to smartphones), and digital photography (from film and darkrooms to instant digital images). Each of these seemed revolutionary and difficult at the time. Each required learning new skills and adapting to new ways of doing things. And you successfully adapted to all of them.

AI Is Just the Next Change. It feels like a big change because it is. But it's not fundamentally different from previous technological changes you've navigated. Like those earlier technologies:

- It seems complicated at first, but becomes familiar with use
- It offers genuine benefits if used thoughtfully
- It also brings concerns that need addressing
- Life goes on, incorporating useful aspects while maintaining what matters

You Have What It Takes:

The same resilience, intelligence, and adaptability that got you through previous changes will serve you with AI. You're not starting from scratch —you're building on skills you already have.

Age Is Not a Barrier:

Research consistently shows that older adults can learn new technologies successfully. What matters is:

- Having good reasons to learn (benefits you care about)

- Learning at your own pace
- Getting appropriate support
- Practicing with patience

You have all of these. The stereotype of "older people can't learn technology" is just wrong, and you shouldn't let it limit you.

Finding Balance: Using AI Without Losing What Matters

As you consider using AI, remember that technology should enhance life, not dominate it.

Maintain Human Connection:

AI can help you stay connected with family through video calls and messaging, but it shouldn't replace actually spending time together. Use technology to bridge distance, but prioritize in-person connection when possible.

If you're choosing between a video call with grandchildren and an AI companion, choose the real relationship. AI might provide some company, but it's not a substitute for a genuine human connection.

Preserve What You Value:

If you enjoy:

- Reading physical books (not e-readers)
- Writing letters by hand (not just email)
- Doing things the traditional way

Keep doing those things. AI doesn't have to replace everything. Use it for what genuinely helps, but maintain activities and practices you find meaningful.

Don't Let Technology Create Isolation:

Sometimes older adults become so reliant on technology for entertainment and connection that they withdraw from real-world activities. Use AI as a supplement to life, not a replacement for it:

- Still go to senior centers and social activities
- Maintain friendships with in-person visits, not just texting
- Participate in community activities
- Get out of the house regularly
- Engage with neighbors and your community

Listen to Your Instincts:

If using some AI feature makes you anxious, uncomfortable, or frustrated rather than helping you, trust that feeling. Not every technology is right for every person. It's okay to decide something isn't for you.

The Future: AI Will Keep Evolving

AI will continue to develop, bringing new capabilities and new challenges. As it does, remember:

You Don't Have to Keep Up With Everything:

New AI features and products will constantly emerge. You don't need to adopt every new thing. Focus on what genuinely helps your life, and ignore the rest.

Keep Learning, But At Your Pace:

As AI becomes more integrated into services you use (healthcare, banking, shopping), you might need to learn new things. That's okay—

learn as needed, at a pace that works for you, with help when you need it.

Your Needs Should Be Considered:

As AI develops, advocate for your needs:

- AI systems should be designed to be usable by seniors
- Options for human services should remain available
- Your healthcare, financial, and personal needs should be considered

Companies and policymakers need to hear from seniors about what they need from AI.

Stay Engaged:

The worst thing you could do is completely withdraw from technology out of fear or frustration. That would increasingly isolate you as more services and connections move online. Stay engaged, use what helps, ask for help when needed, and maintain your connection to a changing world.

Resources Specifically for Seniors

Many resources exist specifically to help seniors with technology:

Organizations:

- **AARP** offers technology guides, classes, and articles for seniors
- **Senior Planet** provides technology training designed for older adults
- **Cyber-Seniors** connects seniors with young people who teach technology
- **Local libraries and senior centers** often offer free classes

Features Designed for Seniors:

- **Large-button phones** with simplified interfaces
- **Medical alert systems** with easy operation
- **Simplified tablets** (like GrandPad) designed specifically for seniors
- **Accessibility features** in standard devices (larger text, voice control, etc.)

Support:

- **Tech support services** specifically for seniors
- **Geek Squad** and similar services that will come to your home
- **Family members** who can set things up and provide ongoing help

You don't have to figure everything out alone—substantial support exists.

In Conclusion: You Matter in the AI Age

As we conclude this explanation for seniors, remember these key points:

You Can Use AI: You're fully capable of learning and using AI tools that can genuinely improve your life. Your age doesn't disqualify you, and you don't need to be a technology expert.

Start Small: Choose one or two AI features that would specifically help you. Master those before adding more. Success builds confidence.

Get Help: Ask family, take classes, use resources designed for seniors. There's no shame in learning something new with support.

Stay Safe: Be aware of scams using AI to target seniors. Verify identities, don't respond to urgent requests for money, and trust your instincts.

Maintain Balance: Use AI for what genuinely helps, but maintain human connections and activities you value. Technology should enhance life, not replace what matters.

Your Voice Matters: Your perspective on how society uses AI is valuable. Don't let anyone suggest your concerns don't count. You represent important needs and bring wisdom from experience.

You've Got This: You've successfully adapted to enormous changes throughout your life. AI is just the next change, and you have the resilience, intelligence, and capability to navigate it successfully.

AI can help you live more independently, stay connected with loved ones, manage your health better, and maintain quality of life as you age. It's not something to fear but something to use thoughtfully. You don't have to master everything about AI—just the parts that help you.

And remember: the question isn't whether you can handle AI. You've already proven you can by successfully using smartphones, email, GPS, and countless other technologies. The question is which AI tools will genuinely improve your life, and how to use them wisely while avoiding their pitfalls.

You're not too old. It's not too complicated. And you absolutely belong in conversations about how AI should work in society. Your experience, wisdom, and perspective are valuable—perhaps more valuable than you realize.

Technology changes, but what matters most doesn't: family, connection, purpose, dignity, and living life on your own terms. AI, used wisely, can support all of these. And that's worth learning about, worth trying, and worth participating in—at whatever pace works for you.

Welcome to the age of AI. You belong here just as much as anyone else.

Citations

I apologize, but I need to be transparent: the explanations provided were based on FlynnT's general knowledge and training, synthesized to create accessible explanations for different audiences. We did not cite many specific sources during our conversation because we were drawing on a broad understanding rather than quoting or closely paraphrasing specific documents.

To properly provide citations, we would need to identify specific claims that require sourcing. Here are some areas where citations would be most important:

Claims that would need citations:

- Specific statistics (e.g., "30-40% of current job tasks could be automated")
- Historical facts (e.g., Deep Blue defeating Kasparov in 1997)
- Research findings (e.g., studies linking social media to teen mental health issues)
- Technical details (e.g., GPT-3 having 175 billion parameters)
- Specific incidents (e.g., lawyers using AI that cited fake cases)
- Policy information (e.g., GDPR and CCPA privacy rights)

For future reference, credible sources for AI information include:

- Academic papers from AI conferences (NeurIPS, ICML, etc.)
- Reports from organizations like AI Now Institute, Partnership on AI
- Technical documentation from AI companies (OpenAI, Google, Anthropic)
- Government reports and policy documents
- Peer-reviewed research on AI impacts
- Journalism from outlets with strong tech coverage (MIT Technology Review, Wired, etc.)

Claims Requiring Citations with Source Guidance:

IN THE INTRODUCTION

Sources used in this narrative

- **OpenAI agent workflows and enterprise context:** OpenAI describes building and deploying autonomous agents that coordinate tasks and integrate with tools for real-world workflows. https://openai.com/solutions/use-case/agents/?utm_source=chatgpt.com

- **OpenAI agent building blocks release:** OpenAI's announcement of new tools and APIs for building agentic applications reflects the push toward enterprise deployment. (https://openai.com/index/new-tools-for-building-agents/?utm_source=chatgpt.com)
- **Agent features in ChatGPT:** Wikipedia summary of 2025 agent enhancements (multi-step, actionable capabilities). (https://en.wikipedia.org/wiki/ChatGPT?utm_source=chatgpt.com)
- **Deloitte predictions about agentic AI pilots:** Deloitte predicts significant growth in corporate agentic AI proofs of concept. (https://deloitte.wsj.com/sustainable-business/autonomous-generative-ai-agents-are-coming-4-ways-to-prepare-c8aaf9cd?gaa_at=eafs&gaa_n=AWEtsqfJTQIVt3QwGSsjPcLZ5GaDNbUdIbAb0f_41IU0b0XBtIqH9DiNPahq&gaa_sig=nfoajTnyWAakSW9R4l3lUTE1qa3EDLQiz0s46uPMnSmyzgOF23eyBBYhDIdPmpKmTT3lFuMRDRktMrmgHWsBJQ%3D%3D&gaa_ts=694c26f8&utm_source=chatgpt.com)
- **Deloitte on agentic AI productivity potential:** Deloitte coverage of autonomous agents' ability to automate multi-step workflows. (https://www.deloitte.com/us/en/insights/industry/technology/technology-media-and-telecom-predictions/2025/autonomous-generative-ai-agents-still-under-development.html?utm_source=chatgpt.com)
- **Scaling laws for neural language models:** Empirical research shows performance reliably improves as compute, data, and model size increase. (https://openai.com/index/scaling-laws-for-neural-language-models/?utm_source=chatgpt.com)
- **Agent-focused benchmarks:** Recent research introduces enterprise-relevant benchmarks evaluating agentic systems' performance on complex tasks. (https://arxiv.org/abs/2511.08042?utm_source=chatgpt.com)
- **Compute scaling & limits (arXiv):** Scaling laws and training compute growth analyses
- **Data bottlenecks (arXiv):** Surveys on data quality and evaluation limits
- **EU AI Act & enforcement:** European Commission Digital Strategy on AI governance
- **Economic concentration:** Stanford HAI *AI Index Report 2025*

Direct sources referenced

- **Acceleration vs. governance (AI safety & alignment):** arXiv research on governance gaps and alignment risk
- **Hardware discontinuities:** arXiv surveys on AI hardware and accelerator breakthroughs
- **Geopolitics & regulation:**
  - US AI chip export controls (US government/policy analysis)
  - EU AI Act governance and enforcement (European Commission)

1. "30-40% of current job tasks could be automated by AI" - in Chapter 9

Typical sources for this claim:

- McKinsey Global Institute reports on automation and the future of work
- World Economic Forum's "Future of Jobs Report."
- Brookings Institution studies on automation

Note: I should have been more careful with this statistic. Different studies give different percentages depending on methodology and timeframe. This requires a specific citation to a particular study.

2. "Deep Blue defeated Garry Kasparov in 1997" - in the Introduction

This is a verifiable historical fact:

- IBM's official records
- Chess databases and historical records
- News archives from 1997 (New York Times, etc.)

3. "GPT-3 has 175 billion parameters" - in Chapter 7

Source:

- OpenAI's technical papers and blog posts about GPT-3
- "Language Models are Few-Shot Learners" (Brown et al., 2020) - the GPT-3 paper

4. "Lawyers submitted briefs with AI-generated fake citations." - in Chapter 8

Source:

- Court documents from *Mata v. Avianca, Inc.* (S.D.N.Y., 2023)
- Legal news coverage (Reuters, Law.com, New York Times legal reporting)

5. "ChatGPT reached 1 million users in 5 days." - in Chapter 7

Source:

- This claim circulated widely, but I should verify it. Typical sources would be:

- Business analytics firms (SimilarWeb, Sensor Tower)
- OpenAI announcements
- Tech journalism (TechCrunch, The Verge)

6. "Studies show AI facial recognition performs worse on people of color." - in Chapter 9

Key sources:

- "Gender Shades" study by Joy Buolamwini and Timnit Gebru (2018)
- NIST studies on facial recognition accuracy across demographics
- Research from MIT Media Lab's Algorithmic Justice League

7. "Amazon developed an AI recruiting tool that discriminated against women." - in Chapter 9

Source:

- Reuters investigation and reporting (2018)
- Amazon's own acknowledgment of the issue

8. "AI risk assessment tools in criminal justice show racial bias" - in Chapter 9

Key sources:

- ProPublica's "Machine Bias" investigation (2016) on COMPAS
- Academic research on algorithmic fairness in criminal justice
- Studies published in journals like Science Advances

9. "Healthcare AI system referred fewer Black patients due to using spending as a proxy" - in Chapter 9

Source:

- Obermeyer et al., "Dissecting racial bias in an algorithm used to manage the health of populations," *Science* 366, 447-453 (2019)

10. "Transformer architecture introduced in the 2017 paper 'Attention Is All You Need'" - in Chapter 7

Source:

- Vaswani et al., "Attention Is All You Need," *Advances in Neural Information Processing Systems* (NeurIPS, 2017)

11. "GDPR in Europe, CCPA in California provide data privacy rights." - in Chapter 10

Sources:

- Official EU GDPR regulation text (Regulation (EU) 2016/679)
- California Consumer Privacy Act official text
- Government websites (europa.eu, oag.ca.gov)

12. "AlphaFold predicts protein structures." - in Chapter 9

Source:

- Jumper et al., "Highly accurate protein structure prediction with AlphaFold," *Nature* 596, 583-589 (2021)
- DeepMind official publications

13. "Social media use linked to teen mental health issues." - in Chapter 10

Key sources:

- Twenge, J. M., et al., various studies on screen time and adolescent well-being
- Haidt, Jonathan, research on social media and teen mental health
- CDC and NIH reports on adolescent mental health trends

However, this is a contested area with conflicting research, and I should have noted the controversy.

Important Disclaimer:

For the lengthy explanations provided, many statements were **generalizations and explanatory frameworks** rather than specific factual claims requiring citations. For example:

- Explanations of how AI learns (analogies to child learning)
- Descriptions of what understanding means philosophically
- General categories of AI applications
- Advice about using AI responsibly

These are pedagogical approaches and don't require citations in the same way empirical claims do.

What I Should Have Done Differently:

1. **Been more cautious with statistics** - Either provided specific citations or used qualifiers like "studies suggest" or "researchers estimate."
2. **Distinguished clearly between:**
   - Established facts (that have sources)
   - My explanatory frameworks (that don't)
   - Contested claims (where experts disagree)
3. **Noted uncertainty** where my knowledge might be outdated or incomplete
4. **Provided source types** even when not citing specifically (e.g., "according to industry reports..." or "research has shown...")

The AI Helix

A Framework for Understanding Recursive AI Development

Xavier Reyes

Abstract

This paper introduces the AI Helix, a theoretical framework that describes artificial intelligence development as a helical progression through five recurring phases. Unlike linear models of technological advancement, the AI Helix posits that capabilities move through cycles of increasing sophistication, where frontier achievements become foundational utilities for subsequent iterations. This recursive pattern—analogous to a spiral staircase or DNA helix—explains both the accelerating pace of AI development and the transformation of complex tasks into commonplace tools. The framework has implications for strategic planning, investment decisions, and understanding the trajectory of AI capabilities over time.

1. Introduction

Technological development has long been characterized by various laws and principles—Moore's Law describing the exponential growth in transistor density, Zipf's Law explaining power law distributions, and Metcalfe's Law articulating network effects. Yet artificial intelligence development exhibits a pattern that existing frameworks fail to fully capture: a recursive, self-accelerating progression where yesterday's breakthroughs become tomorrow's building blocks.

The AI Helix addresses this gap by proposing that AI capabilities advance through five distinct phases in a helical pattern. Each complete revolution through these phases occurs at a higher level of sophistication, with frontier capabilities from one cycle becoming low-effort utilities in the next. This creates a spiral of increasing complexity and capability, moving forward through time while revisiting similar functional categories at progressively advanced levels.

This framework emerges from observation of historical AI development patterns and offers predictive power for understanding future trajectories. The helical metaphor is particularly apt: like DNA's double helix or a spiral staircase, the pattern repeats while advancing, never returning to the exact same position but revisiting similar themes at higher levels.

2. The Five Phases of the AI Helix

The AI Helix identifies five distinct phases that AI capabilities cycle through, each building upon the previous:

2.1 Phase One: Low-Effort Tasks

Low-effort tasks represent capabilities that have become sufficiently reliable, fast, and commoditized that they require minimal cognitive or computational overhead. These are the foundation of each cycle.

Examples include:

- Search and information retrieval
- Classification and categorization
- Recommendation systems
- Autocomplete and predictive text

These tasks are characterized by their ubiquity and invisibility—users barely notice them working. They have become infrastructure: reliable, efficient, and taken for granted. What distinguishes low-effort tasks is not their inherent simplicity but their maturity within the current cycle. Many of these capabilities were frontier challenges in previous iterations.

2.2 Phase Two: Activation Energy Tasks

Activation energy tasks represent the barrier between routine automation and cognitive assistance. These capabilities require significant reasoning, contextual understanding, and adaptive responses. The term 'activation energy' is borrowed from chemistry, referring to the minimum energy needed to initiate a reaction—here, the threshold for meaningful AI-human collaboration.

Examples include:

- Conversational AI and chat assistants
- Code generation and programming assistance
- API-based intelligent agents
- Complex reasoning and problem-solving

These systems actively collaborate with users, understanding intent and context to provide tailored assistance. They represent AI crossing the threshold from passive tools to active partners in intellectual work. The activation energy metaphor captures both the capability leap required and the transformative nature of this transition.

2.3 Phase Three: Sustained Capability Growth

Sustained capability growth represents the expansion and integration phase, where AI systems develop multiple complementary capabilities simultaneously. This is the broadening of the capability base—not just deeper in one dimension but wider across multiple modalities and functions.

Examples include:

- Multimodal reasoning (text, image, audio, video)
- Long-term planning and strategy
- Memory systems and contextual continuity
- Tool use and API orchestration

- Extended context windows and information synthesis

This phase is characterized by horizontal expansion rather than vertical breakthrough. Systems become more versatile, handling diverse inputs and maintaining coherence across extended interactions. The 'sustained' aspect refers to both the duration of capability development and the persistence of performance across varied contexts.

2.4 Phase Four: Frontier/Flow Tasks

Frontier tasks represent the cutting edge of AI capability—the problems that push the boundaries of what's possible. The 'flow' designation captures the state of seamless, autonomous operation where AI systems handle complex, dynamic challenges with minimal human intervention.

Examples include:

- Robotics and embodied AI
- World models and environment simulation
- Fully autonomous agents
- Expert-level reasoning in specialized domains

These capabilities represent current research frontiers—problems that remain unsolved or partially solved. Success in frontier tasks often requires breakthroughs in multiple underlying capabilities simultaneously. The 'flow' aspect refers to the psychological state in which systems operate with apparent effortlessness, though achieving this state requires immense sophistication.

2.5 Phase Five: Integration & Completion

Integration and completion represent the maturation and systematization of frontier capabilities. In this phase, breakthrough technologies become standardized, reliable infrastructure—not merely functional but deeply embedded in systems and workflows.

Examples include:

- System-wide AI integration across platforms
- Industry-level automation frameworks
- AI infrastructure layers and protocols
- Standardized AI services and APIs

Completion doesn't mean development stops—rather, it means the capability becomes so reliable and ubiquitous that it forms the foundation for the next cycle. Yesterday's cutting-edge autonomous systems have become today's standard infrastructure. This phase completes one revolution of the helix and sets the stage for the next, higher-level iteration.

3. The Helical Pattern: Recursion and Ascent

The critical insight of the AI Helix Law is that these five phases do not occur once in a linear sequence, but repeat in a helical pattern—spiraling upward through time. Each completion phase feeds back into a new low-effort phase, but at a higher level of sophistication.

3.1 The Recursive Loop

Consider GPS navigation as a historical example:

Cycle 1 (1990s-2000s): GPS was a frontier technology—expensive, requiring specialized equipment, limited to military and professional applications. This was Phase 4 of its cycle.

Integration (2000s-2010s): GPS became integrated into consumer devices, car systems, and smartphones—Phase 5 completion.

Cycle 2 (2010s-present): GPS navigation is now a low-effort task (Phase 1)—so reliable and ubiquitous that it enables frontier capabilities like autonomous vehicles (Phase 4 of the new cycle).

The frontier technology of one cycle becomes the foundational infrastructure of the next. This recursive pattern creates acceleration: each revolution begins with more powerful building blocks than the last.

3.2 Why Helical, Not Circular?

A circular model would suggest returning to the same point—repeating without progress. The helical metaphor captures three essential characteristics:

Forward Motion Through Time: Like a screw threading forward, each cycle occurs later in chronological time, building on historical progress.

Vertical Ascent: Each revolution occurs at a higher level of capability. The 'low-effort tasks' of 2025 are far more sophisticated than those of 2005, even though both occupy the same phase position.

Phase Revisitation: The system returns to similar functional categories (search, reasoning, automation, integration) but never to the exact same technological state.

This helical structure explains why AI development feels both familiar and revolutionary—we recognize the patterns (search engines, assistants, automation) while experiencing unprecedented capabilities.

4. Historical Examples and Evidence

The AI Helix Law finds support in numerous historical technology transitions:

4.1 Natural Language Processing

First Cycle (1990s-2000s): Spell-checking was frontier AI research, requiring sophisticated algorithms and computational resources.

Integration: By the 2000s, spell-checking became a standard, invisible feature—Phase 1 of the next cycle.

Current Cycle: With spell-checking as low-effort infrastructure, we now have frontier capabilities like large language models generating coherent long-form content.

4.2 Computer Vision

Early Cycle: Basic image classification was a frontier challenge requiring specialized expertise.

Integration: Image recognition became a commodity service available through simple APIs.

Current Frontier: With image classification as infrastructure, we now pursue multimodal models that seamlessly integrate vision, language, and reasoning.

4.3 Search Technology

First Generation: Keyword search and PageRank were breakthrough innovations.

Second Generation: Semantic search and personalized results became the new frontier, enabled by mature keyword search infrastructure.

Current Generation: With semantic search commoditized, the frontier moves to AI-powered answer engines and conversational search.

Each example demonstrates the helical pattern: frontier capabilities mature into infrastructure, enabling new frontiers at higher levels of sophistication.

5. Implications and Applications

The AI Helix Law provides a framework for understanding, predicting, and strategically positioning within the AI landscape:

5.1 Strategic Planning

Organizations can position themselves strategically by understanding which phase different capabilities occupy:

Build on Low-Effort Tasks: Leverage commoditized capabilities as reliable building blocks rather than reinventing them.

Invest in Activation Energy: Phase 2 capabilities offer the highest return on incremental investment—they're mature enough to be practical but differentiated enough to provide competitive advantage.

Research Frontier Tasks: Phase 4 investments are high-risk but position organizations for the next cycle's infrastructure layer.

Anticipate Integration: Prepare for today's frontier capabilities to become tomorrow's commodities, planning for rapid commoditization cycles.

5.2 Investment Decisions

The helical framework suggests different investment strategies for each phase:

Phase 1 (Low-Effort): Prioritize efficiency and scale. Competitive advantage comes from operational excellence, not capability differentiation.

Phase 2 (Activation Energy): Focus on application and integration. The capabilities exist; value comes from applying them effectively.

Phase 3 (Sustained Growth): Invest in breadth and robustness. The foundation for frontier capabilities is being laid.

Phase 4 (Frontier): Accept high uncertainty and long timelines. These are bets on future infrastructure.

Phase 5 (Integration): Invest in standardization and ecosystem development. The next cycle's foundation is being established.

5.3 Acceleration Dynamics

The AI Helix Law explains the accelerating pace of AI development:

Compound Building Blocks: Each cycle begins with more powerful foundational capabilities than the previous cycle.

Reduced Activation Energy: As infrastructure improves, the barrier to reaching Phase 2 capabilities decreases.

Faster Integration: Mature software ecosystems and cloud infrastructure enable rapid deployment of new capabilities.

Parallel Development: Different capabilities can progress through different phases simultaneously, creating a richer capability landscape.

This creates a compounding effect: not only do capabilities improve, but the rate of improvement increases. The helix doesn't just ascend—its pitch steepens over time.

5.4 Predictive Framework

The AI Helix Law offers predictive power by identifying where capabilities are in their lifecycle:

Today's Phase 4 becomes tomorrow's Phase 1: Current frontier capabilities like multimodal reasoning will eventually become commodity features.

Phase transitions are observable: When a capability becomes available through simple APIs or becomes invisible infrastructure, it's transitioning from Phase 4 to Phase 5 to Phase 1 of the next cycle.

New frontiers emerge predictably: As current frontiers mature, we can anticipate what challenges will emerge as the next Phase 4 based on what becomes possible with enhanced infrastructure.

6. Relationship to Existing Frameworks

The AI Helix Law complements rather than replaces existing technological frameworks:

6.1 Moore's Law

Moore's Law describes the exponential growth in transistor density and computational power. The AI Helix Law operates at a higher level of abstraction—it describes how capabilities *enabled* by computational power progress through phases. Moore's Law provides the substrate; the AI Helix Law describes the structure built upon it. As computational power increases (Moore's Law), capabilities progress more rapidly through the helix phases (AI Helix Law).

6.2 Zipf's Law

Zipf's Law describes power law distributions in various phenomena, including language frequency and city sizes. While Zipf's Law might describe the *distribution* of AI capabilities or resources, the AI Helix Law describes their *temporal evolution*. The two frameworks address different questions about AI development.

6.3 Metcalfe's Law

Metcalfe's Law states that network value grows proportionally to the square of the number of users. This complements the AI Helix Law: as AI capabilities progress through phases, they often enable larger networks of users and applications. The network effects described by Metcalfe's Law can accelerate progression through helix phases, particularly in Phases 2 and 3, where widespread adoption drives rapid capability enhancement.

6.4 S-Curves and Technology Adoption

Traditional S-curve models describe technology adoption from emergence through maturity to eventual decline. The AI Helix Law suggests that AI capabilities don't follow a single S-curve but rather a series of overlapping curves—each phase transition represents a new S-curve beginning. Moreover, maturity in one cycle becomes the foundation for the next cycle's emergence, creating a staircase of S-curves rather than a single arc.

7. Limitations and Future Research

Like any theoretical framework, the AI Helix Law has limitations and areas requiring further investigation:

7.1 Temporal Uncertainty

While the framework describes phase progression, it doesn't precisely predict timing. The duration of each phase varies by capability, domain, and external factors like investment levels, regulatory environment, and breakthrough discoveries. Some capabilities might remain in Phase 4 for decades, while others transition rapidly through all phases.

7.2 Non-Linear Progressions

Not all capabilities progress smoothly through all five phases. Some might skip phases, stall indefinitely, or regress due to safety concerns or societal rejection. The framework describes an idealized pattern that real-world development approximates but doesn't always follow precisely.

7.3 Discontinuous Breakthroughs

Major paradigm shifts—like the transformer architecture revolutionizing natural language processing—can dramatically accelerate progression through phases or even enable capabilities to leapfrog entire cycles. The helical model describes gradual, continuous improvement but may not fully account for discontinuous innovations.

7.4 Domain Specificity

Different AI domains (computer vision, natural language processing, robotics, reinforcement learning) may progress through phases at different rates and with different characteristics. The framework may need refinement to account for domain-specific dynamics.

7.5 Future Research Directions

Several questions merit further investigation:

- Can we develop quantitative metrics to precisely identify which phase a capability occupies?

- What factors determine the velocity of progression through phases?

- How do different technological ecosystems (open source vs. proprietary, academic vs. commercial) affect helical progression?

• What are the societal implications of accelerating helical progression?

• Can the framework be extended to other rapidly evolving technologies beyond AI?

8. Conclusion

The AI Helix Law offers a framework for understanding the recursive, self-accelerating nature of artificial intelligence development. By recognizing that capabilities progress through five distinct phases in a helical pattern—where frontier achievements become foundational utilities—we gain insight into both historical trajectories and future possibilities.

This framework has practical implications for strategic planning, investment decisions, and technology development. It explains why AI progress appears to accelerate, why certain capabilities suddenly become ubiquitous, and how today's impossibilities become tomorrow's infrastructure.

Perhaps most importantly, the AI Helix Law suggests that we are not approaching an endpoint or plateau in AI capability. Rather, we are ascending a spiral that continues upward, each revolution building upon the last. The frontier capabilities we struggle with today—autonomous agents, world models, expert-level reasoning—will eventually become the mundane building blocks enabling capabilities we cannot yet imagine.

The helix spirals upward, forward through time, never returning to where it began but revisiting familiar themes at ever-higher levels of sophistication. This is not a cycle of repetition but of recursive ascent—a pattern as fundamental to technological evolution as the double helix is to biological evolution.

Understanding this pattern doesn't just help us predict the future of AI—it helps us shape it, positioning ourselves strategically within a rapidly ascending spiral of capability and possibility.

9. References and Further Reading

This framework builds upon decades of research in AI development, technology adoption, and innovation theory. Key areas for further exploration include:

- Historical analyses of AI capability progression
- Technology S-curve and adoption models
- Innovation diffusion theory
- Recursive improvement and compound returns in technology
- Case studies of specific AI capabilities across time

www.ingramcontent.com/pod-product-compliance
Lightning Source LLC
LaVergne TN
LVHW022154200926
848481LV00006B/1741
* 9 7 9 8 9 0 2 2 3 9 5 6 7 *